THE SEXUALITY OF LATINAS

Edited by
Norma Alarcón
Ana Castillo
Cherríe Moraga

Third Woman Press
Berkeley

PS 508 .H57 S49 1993

The sexuality of Latinas

Copyright © 1993 by Third Woman Press

All rights reserved under International and
Pan American Copyright Conventions.
Published by Third Woman Press.
Manufactured in the United States of
America.

Typeset by Cragmont Publications, Oakland,
Calif.
Printed and bound by McNaughton & Gunn,
Saline, Mich.

No part of this book may be reproduced by
any mechanical, photographic, or electronic
process, or in the form of a phonographic
recording, nor may it be stored in a retrieval
system, transmitted, or otherwise copied for
public or private use, except for brief
quotations in critical articles or reviews,
without the prior written permission of the
publisher. Address inquiries to: Third Woman
Press; Ethnic Studies, Dwinelle Hall 3412,
University of California, Berkeley, CA 94720

First printing 1993
93 94 95 96 97   10 9 8 7 6 5 4 3 2 1

ISBN 0-943219-0-00

This book would not have been possible without the help of the Third Woman Collective and especially Ana Coronado, María Hernández, Rosa Johnson and Magali Zúñiga. Thank you.

Contents

Introduction   8

Poetry

Adela Alonso
    Tanto Tiempo   11

Cordelia Chávez Candelaria
    Segments   16
    The Fall   17
    Sin amor   18

Sandra Cisneros
    Down There   19

Rosina Conde
    Los sueños de Juana   24

Lucha Corpi
    Márgenes—seis   33
    Márgenes—nueve   34
    Márgenes—once   35

Barbara Brinson Curiel
    Ciudadano de mis sueños   36

Luzma Umpierre
    Transcendence   38

Sylviana Wood
    Sweet Revenge   40

Prose

Adela Alonso
    Virgencita, danos chance   43

Elvia Alvarado
    Don't be Afraid, Gringo (Excerpts)   47

Julia Álvarez
    The Summer Of The Future   53

Gloria Anzaldúa
    La historia de la marimacho   64

Denise Chávez
    The Face of an Angel (Excerpts)   69

Claudia Colindres
    A Letter To My Mother   73

Erlinda Gonzáles-Berry
    Conversaciones con Sergio   80

Rosalee Gurrola
    Woolworth's Bra   83

Arcelia Ponce
    La preferida   85

Sonia Rivera-Valdés
    Las historias prohibidas de Marta
    Veneranda (fragmento)   90

Victoria Alegría Rosales
    To All Women Who Have Traveled
    the Same Road As I   99

Mary Siqueiros
    First Time   101
    My Other Self (Journal entry, Fall 1970)   104

Carmen Tafolla
    Federico y Elfiria   105

Drama

Ana María Simo
    What Do You See?   113

Essays/Reviews

Peggy Job
    La sexualidad en la narrativa femenina
    mexicana 1970-1987   120

Juanita Luna Lawhn
    Impediments to Women's Self-Definition   134

Yvonne Yarbro-Bejarano
    Primer encuentro de lesbianas feministas
    latinoamericanas y caribeñas   143

Ana Castillo
    The Distortion of Desire   147

Cherríe Moraga
    Algo secretamente amado   151
    The Obedient Daughter   157

Alvina Quintana
    La lucha continúa   163

Lourdes Torres
    Risking All for Margarita   166

Art

Juana Alicia
    Xochiquetzal   112

Cecilia Álvarez
    Los eternos sacrificios   159

Santa Barraza
    Mother Looks On While Vulture Preys On Us 87
    Coatlicue 153

Rita Chávez
    Who Can We Be? 103

Marina Gutiérrez
    Sisters 55

Ester Hernández
    Renée La troquera back cover
    La Virgen de Guadalupe 42

Enedina Cásarez-Vásquez
    Como semos mujeres, siempre nos
        verán así front cover

Bibliography

Norma Alarcón
    Chicana Writers and Critics in a Social
    Context: Towards a Contemporary
    Bibliography 169

Peggy Job
    Narradoras mexicanas contemporáneas,
    1970-1987 179

Contributors 185

Introduction

In 1984 *Third Woman* journal decided to pursue the publication of a Chicana/Latina lesbian issue. However, such an issue never materialized. In part this is due to the fact that very few professional writers—be they creative or critical—have actively pursued a lesbian political identity. Among creative writers one can highlight the work of Gloria Anzaldúa, Cherríe Moraga, Mirtha Quintanales, and Luz María Umpierre. More recently, among our critics, Luz María Umpierre and Yvonne Yarbro-Bejarano have been actively pursuing a lesbian critical perspective. This particular state of affairs may not have become so apparent had we not decided to explore the field so as to produce a Chicana/Latina lesbian issue. Of course, it is still the case that many a Latina who wants to pursue a political and literary lesbian identity usually does so outside of her own ethnic community. As a result we made the decision to forego a special lesbian issue and instead present her voice as an integral part of the Latina experience—from the actively heterosexual, to the celibate, to the secretly sexual, to the politically visible lesbian. In this book then, the Latina lesbian is allowed to express the myriad aspects of her identity in relation to the same forces that have shaped her hermanas.

Once the range of contributors was established, we debated what constituted a submission that could be considered thematically sexual. Thus, we had a lively discussion with respect to the difference between "gender" themes and "sexual" themes. In brief, we agreed that the former leaned heavily on a theoretical vision that often gave us an abstract or academic vocabulary, while the later relied on the concrete sexual image that depicted our practices and our emotional responses to them. Clearly, it is impossible, in many instances, to avoid abstract conceptualization, especially with regard to work written in Spanish by middle class Latinas, (See Job's essay in this book.) The Latin American *burguesía*, in general, has often relied on French and other underground materials for its sexual/erotic literature, with few exceptions. In a sense, then, we speak of a taboo among the *burguesía* where sexuality as an explicit theme was limited to the realm of theory or covert metaphor. Among the poplar sector, however, sexuality has often been a brutal daily affair without record. As such, the working-class or campesina population only now begins the grueling self-examination of our five-hundred-year-old status as silenced labor and sexual being.

One can, for example, point to the fact that neither Latin American nor U.S. laws protect poor women with unwanted pregnancies. Underaged Latinas are affected drastically because of government policy that does not protect them at all against unplanned pregnancies as well. Even now in the last decade of the twentieth century no safe and effective contraceptive has been developed. Also, in the 1970s it was well publicized, after the fact, that many U.S. women of color, poor and incarcerated women were sterilized without their knowledge. Even with the AIDS plague affecting all of society our federal government finds it difficult to put an emergency plan into action. Making matters worse, men still persist in their archaic attitude against the standard use of condoms. To further demonstrate the fact that women's sexuality is closely tied to patriarchal law, none of the rights granted to a heterosexual married couple are extended to the committed lesbian couple. Indeed, the rights of a lesbian to pursue her own lifestyle are not guaranteed in our society.

Our sexuality has been hidden, subverted, distorted within the "sacred" walls of the "familia"—be it myth or reality— and within the even more privatized walls of our bedrooms. Like many women, our understanding of our sexual desire too often comes through the reality of sexual violence. In the journey to the love of female self and each other we are ultimately forced to confront father, brother, and god (and mother as his agent).

In view of this historical repression, with the exception of some academic essays, submissions for this book were slow to come. Deadlines were extended and finally ignored as we began the task of personally contacting women whom we knew were capable of writing sexually thematic pieces and would not shy away from using their own name. As it is, several pieces in this anthology are pseudonymous, yet this is mitigated by the fact that some of the strongest voices, with their own name attached, are also the youngest amongst us—the rawest, the less trained, and those with the least to lose. In any case this project became a testimony to the long-censored, non-white, non-protestant working-class woman living within a major world power.

We hope that this book is not an isolated effort to begin the discussion of our sexuality and we encourage and look forward to the future publications that explicitly view sexuality and gender at the forefront of the sociopolitical struggle of Latinas in all levels of society.

Norma Alarcón
Ana Castillo
Cherríe Moraga

Adela Alonso

Tanto Tiempo

me excita verte junto a Armando
    desnuda
  su pene parado, camote con leche
    te lo mete
      dulce y tierno
        como es él
        como eres tú
por fin estamos los tres aquí en mi cama
    como lo soñé tantas veces
Armando chupa una chichi tuya
  yo la otra
tus pechos henchidos destilan placeres

        y más abajo
        tus labios

                por la talydomina
                  nací chiquita
                    como almendrita

                sólo mis pechos
              enormes mangos maduros
                arqueaban mi
                  tallo verde y fino
          eran una aberración en mi cuerpo
                me los vendaba
                  los aplastaba

tanto tiempo en probar
    ¿en probar qué?
        ¿y a quién?
una definición cultural
    homo-hetero-bi
    tantos años

tantos años de probar que eres mujer
    ¿para qué?
        ¿para quién?
congelada en tu miedo te lanzabas
    a todos los hombres
    a huevo
penetraspenetepenetraban

                        en aquel viaje se me antojó
                            varias veces
                        me acordé de la película Messidor
                        en que dos chavas al llegar a un
                        campo hacían el amor

                            pero
                            no hallaba cómo decírtelo

hubo puentes entre nosotras—
    Fred, Jordi, Armando
        puentes de deseos
    entre tus pechos y los míos

        brisa embriagada de
        infinita ternura

                      fue horrible Amalia, fue horrible
                      bajamos del edificio
                          los escalones hechos cachitos
                          las paredes de gelatina, ¡ay!

—una vez cuando era niña le pregunté
  a mi mamá si se podían casar dos
  mujeres (porque yo me quería casar
  contigo) . . .
—y ¿qué te dijo?
—que no

yo quería estar siempre contigo

                ¿sabías que mi hermano es
                   homosexual?
                mi mamá llegó a mi casa
                   destruída
                la cobija de su belleza tirada a
                   media calle
                se preguntaba si era su culpa
                   el abandono
                trató de recordar cúando

                      desarmada
                      desolada
                      como una niña

antes del pene
    estuvo este deseo primario—
  el calor de tus pechos
      suaves
          generosos
     tu cinturita
       tu hermosa cara

mi padre
    duro
    con su verga golpeó a mi
        hermano
desnudo
prieto
feo
    su piel morena igual a mi piel
    blanca

la misma sangre

como perrito golpeado
mi hermano llora su amargura
y yo
quieromataralárabeguapísimo
hijodeputagalánquelopatea

    crimen y castigo
piel morena
    desprotegida
llora sobre su pene

que poco supe yo de ti
que poco supe yo de mí

tanto tiempo en reconocer
que en mi destino obraban otras
    manos
que me empujaban al laberinto
tanto tiempo en encontrar mi voz
que ya no es de pito
sino de una campana que
    canta
la música de mi alma
tanto tiempo contenida

déjame ver tus muñecas
    una vez más
déjame sentir la cicatriz
    de la duda
ahora que te siento tan ¡viva!

mis manos descubren tus pechos
    se deslizan por las pesadas curvas
  que como frutas maduras
    coronan tu esbelto cuerpo

y ahí   como lo esperaba

  a flor de piel
anidado entre tus pechos
   tiento un durazno colorado
      blandito
        y dulce

Cordelia Chávez Candelaria

Segments

She peeled the orange tenderly
as if it were a letter from a lover.
Air became tangy citrus mist
caressing every fragrant breath she took.

She pulled the fruity wedge
from its vulnerable whole and sucked
it soft. Fingers of oily sweetness
clung to all she touched, orange prints

separate from the tender hand placing
peel and seed and stringy membrane
into another mass of parts.
Sweet grip on a segment of her life.

Cordelia Chávez Candelaria

The Fall

In that prehistory of our love
When time meant only
Sunwarmth/starlight love
Before consequences weighted
Every tenderness to earth
Mudlike
Your flaws compelled
Like primal signs
Cave paintings etched within me
To show from whence you came
How far with me you traveled
Toward the light.

Then a crisp clear day
And seeing your lover
Grocery sacks weighing her walk
Forced record-keeping on us.

Minutes roll round to duties.
Your smile bothers.
Your hand upon my shoulder
Lies heavy.

Cordelia Chávez Candelaria

Sin amor

Needing arms. Another's.
Lacking warmth. Of touch.
    And whispered flesh caress.
    (Estoy sola.)
Sin the more, you said.
I want. Sin amor
hasta la lengua se cambia.

Sandra Cisneros

Down There

> *At that moment, Little Flower scratched herself*
> *where one never scratches oneself.*
> from "The Smallest Woman in the World"
> —Clarice Lispector

Your poem thinks it's *Bad*.
Because it farts in the bath.
Cracks its knuckles in class.
Grabs its balls in public
and adjusts—one,
then the other—
back and forth like Slinky. No,
more like the motion
of a lava lamp.
You follow me?

Your poem thinks it
cool to pee in the pool.
Waits for the moment
someone's watching before
it sticks a finger up
its nose and licks
it. Your poem's wierd.

The kind that swaggers in like Wayne
or struts its stuff like Rambo.
The kind that learned
to spit at 13 and still
is doing it.

It Blames its bad habits
on the Catholic school.
Picked up words that
snapped like bra straps.
Learned words that ignite
of their own gas
like a butt hole flower.
Fell in love with words
that thudded like stones and sticks.
Or stung like fists.
Or stank like shit
gorillas throw at zoos.

Your poem never washes
its hands after using the can.
Stands around rolling
toilet paper into wet balls
it can toss up on the ceiling
just to watch them stick.
Yuk yuk.

Your poem is a used rubber
sticky on the floor
the next morning,

the black elephant
skin of the testicles,
hairy as kiwi fruit
and silly,

the shaving
stubble against the purity
of porcelain,

one black pubic
hair on the sexy
lip of toilet seat,

the swirl of spit
with a cream of celery
center,

a cigarette
stub sent hissing
to the piss pot,

half-finished
bottles of beer reeking
their yeast incense,

the miscellany of maleness:
nailclippers and keys,
tobacco and ashes,
pennies quarters nickels dimes
and dollars folded into complicated origami,
stub of ticket and pencil and cigarette, and
the crumb of the pockets
all scattered on the Irish
linen of my bedside table.

Oh my little booger,
it's true.

Because someone once
said Don't
do that!
you like to do it.

Baby, I'd like to mention
the tampax you pulled with your teeth
once in a *Playboy* poem*
and found it, darling, not so bloody.
Not so bloody at all, in fact.

---

* John Updike's "Cunts" in *Playboy*, (January 1984), 163.

Hardly blood cousin
except for an unfortunate
association of color
that makes you want to swoon.

Yes,
I want to talk at length about MEN-
struation. Or my period.
Or the rag as you so lovingly put it.
Alright then.

I'd like to mention my rag time.

Gelatinous. Steamy
and lovely to the light to look at
like a good glass of burgundy. Suddenly
I'm artist each month.
The star inside this like a ruby.
Fascinating bits of sticky
I-don't-know-what stuff.
The afterbirth without, the birth.
The gobs of a strawberry jam.
Membrane stretchy like
saliva in your hand

It's important you feel its slickness,
understand the texture isn't bloody at all.
That you don't gush
between the legs. Rather,
it unravels itself like string
from some deep deep center—
like a Russian subatomic submarine,
or better, like a mad Karlov cackling
behind beakers and blooping spirals.
Still with me?

Oh I know, darling,
I'm indulging, but indulge
me if you please.
I find the subject charming.

In fact,
I'd like to dab my fingers
or a swab of tampax
in my inkwell
and write a poem across the wall.
"A Poem of Womanhood"
Now wouldn't that be something?

Words writ in blood. But no,
not blood at all, I told you.
If blood is thicker than water, then
menstruation is thicker than brother-
hood. And the way

it metamorphosizes! Dazzles.
Changing daily
like starlight.
From the first
transparent drop of light
to the fifth day chocolate paste.

I haven't mentioned smell. Think
Persian rug.
But thicker. Think
cello.
But richer.
A sweet exotic snuff
from an ancient prehistoric center.
Dark, distinct,
and excellently
female.

Rosina Conde

Los sueños de Juana

—Para Carlota quien, por su corta
edad, no sabe aún nada de ésto.

I

Miras las estrellas con los ojos espantosamente abiertos
un cuerpo que se mueve al compás de una canción norteña está
    prendido sobre ti.
Sólo tu cabeza permanece clavada a la gleba.
Con la cara entre tu cuello
y su mano lastimando la tuya
introduce un dedo en tu ondulante vagina espumosa.
Te imaginas en el centro de una plataforma:
mil jadeos siguen el ritmo de tu respiración.
Piensas que te observan a través de un monitor
pero no eres tú quien está en la pantalla sino ellos y no
    quieres voltear a verlos.
Te aferras a las estrellas al momento que unos dientes muerden
    tu cuello y el cierre de un pantalón muerde tu pubis.
Ya no es el dedo quien se introduce en tu vagina sino algo
    filoso y duro
te rasga y tus caderas se abren a la fuerza
tus piernas se juntan para evitarlo.
El silencio alarga tu grito
y el cuerpo parece gozar con él prendiéndose de tu cuello como
    perro rabioso.
Sientes frío
un frío insoportable
mas no puedes temblar
porque el cuerpo está enterrándote en la hierba.

II

Otro dice que ya es hora y el cuerpo se levanta.
Tu mano asciende como garfio
hacia tu vientre hasta quedar inmóvil
y tú, clavada al cielo permaneces
sin voltear a ver al nuevo cuerpo que se lanza
a enterrar el garfio entre tu abdomen.
Tus ojos jalan la cabeza
el pecho se expande, se calienta
y escuchas gritos sordos
pero encima de ti no hay nadie
sólo energía sin contorno
una canción norteña se introduce por tus poros

> Pantalón de lana
> chamarra de cuero
> las botas tejanas
> y ancho su sombrero
>
> le dice bonita
> ojos de lucero
> le dice bonita
> boquita de fuego
>
> Contesta cantando
> no tengo luceros
> contesta cantando
> mi boca es de acero
>
> él dice enojado
> yo tengo dinero
> él dice enojado
> tengo lo que quiero

Tu boca se abre al compás de la vagina
y un llanto seco la abandona.
El nuevo cuerpo toca tus carnes comprimidas
se te queda mirando
y pregunta si es ésta la primera vez.
Es entonces cuando ríes y tiemblas y abandonas a las estrellas.

III

Qué rico se duerme en el camión
lo malo es que hay demasiados baches y luego brinca mucho
¿verdad, Juana?
Pero se duerme bien con el movimiento...
Qué almohada tan dura.
Estás embarazada mientras bajas la escalera
una escalera infinita...
Resbalas...
Caes...
Un hospital.
¿Que quién es el padre?
Signo de interrogación.
No lo sabes, no le conoces...
Nunca habías pensado en él
¿verdá, Juana?
Y ahora, por tu egoísmo, has perdido al bebé...
Bebé bé bé é é...
Enfermeras.
Sus caras se distorsionan tras el gran angular.
Y has perdido al bebé bé bé é é
al bebé bé bé é é
¡Pinche bache!, te golpeaste otra vez
¿verdá, Juana?

IV

Volviste en ti llena de tierra
y magullada de las piernas y brazos y senos y cara.
¡A chingar a su madre!, habías contestado
y no supiste en qué momento se habían bajado del auto y
    empezaron
        a golpearte y a picarte las nalgas.
Y allí estás ahora, sentada, inmóvil
con la vista fija en la ventana soñando cosas intangibles
una confusión de sonidos mezclándose con una canción norteña...
Gritos, chasquidos, crujir de hierba seca...
Una mano como garfio posando sobre tu abdomen.

¿En qué estarías pensando entonces, Juana?
Quién sabe
pero recuerdas el silbido del aire de la montaña...
Una canción...

V

Hablas y escuchas, cuchas cuchas
¡estúpida voz como el eco que resuena en la caverna del cráneo!
Lejana, vaga.
No, no eres tú ésa que oyes
eso que dices no lo sientes, no te pertenece
ni ésa esperando de pie desde aquí
desde tu silla de ruedas, bufanda y saco.
Para usted que se atreve a destacar: Colores encendidos...
Lápices labiales y esmalte para uñas...
¿Quiere usted conquistar a un hombre?
¡El milagro!
El novio triunfante y el supremo anhelo...
Tú: vestida de blanco
gasas, tules, perlas, chantillí...
Y te ves desde tu silla tenebrosa, distante
y ahora eres la niña extraviada en el bosque enmedio de la noche
¡y el hada no aparece!
Sólo los príncipes golpeándote con palabras de angustia.
Perdida en los abismos de la locura
sientes los ojos cansados
toda tú estás cansada
duelen la espalda, el corazón
y la silla es dura...
La espalda...
La espalda...
Y el abismo
Y la mona no llega para acostarse y quitar esa música de
    iglesia, la cual te hunde más en la caverna de tu muerte.

La espalda...
La espalda...
Y tu mano como garfio...
Y el silencio en el vacío del sueño lento, pesado...
Una canción norteña se introduce por tus poros....
    él dice enojado
    yo tengo dinero
    él dice enojado
    tengo lo que quiero

VI

Y vas vestida de reina
te miran
aplauden mientras caminas al compás de la marcha.
Tu corona relumbra encandilando.
Las gasas de tu cuerpo vuelan por la noche
saltan por las ventanas.
Sonríes amable mientras te sientas.
¡Qué tenso trono!
Detestas las risas
las miradas morbosas de quienes aplauden.
Las gasas flotan de nuevo escondiendo tu vientre hinchado
bajas la escalera levitando...
(¡si tan sólo hubieras llorado entonces...!)
Tocas el piso de puntas
(¡estarías perdonada, Juana!)
flotando
y caes al abismo
interminablemente, mente mente
te has quedado dormida
¿verdá, Juana?
con tu sonrisa de reina apacible, ible ible
o novia satisfecha, echa echa
con el garfio apuntando hacia tu abdomen

VII

El vientre aún está hinchado
aunque hueco, eco eco
cilicios de amargura reprimen el llanto
y en la oquedad silva el viento.
Estás sola esperando a Alguien
viendo por la ventana imágenes confusas
mientras chillan las cuerdas de una guitarra
pero de nada te sirve llorar ahora, Juana
se acabaron la risa y mirada ingenuas
el culto secreto del amor.
El canto de los grillos
arrulla tu virginidad latente
y el olor de las huele-de-noche
rinde homenaje a tu nueva pasión
porque ahora, Juana
ya no verás las estrellas
ni cortarás más flores
ni pasearás por la ocre montaña en el otoño
ni cruzarás el río como antes
ahora, Juana
arrullarás un feto muerto entre tus brazos
y te secarás hasta pudrirte porque no quieres verte, Juana

VIII

Ha llegado la mona para trasladarse a la cama
las imágenes de la ventana se han vestido de infantil brocado
azul
¡No te rías, Juana!
Calla, la noche es larga . . .
Los caballeros de la Garrotera han jurado vengarte
y recuperar al bebé bé bé é é
Alguien se acerca
y, rodilla en tierra, besa el garfio.

Cubierto de perlas resplandece
calzas, manos, pecho, cuello resplandecen
¡te está cubriendo de besos, Juana!
mas no son los mismos besos y gritas de placer
(porque ahora sí gritas
¿verdá, Juana?
pero nunca habías pensado en ello
¡levanta la falda!, ¿qué esperas?)
el ritmo de tu respiración aumenta
(más sutiles son las caricias)
y te toca toda, oda oda...
mientras musita una canción norteña
¡ja, ja!, ¿qué dijiste, Juana?
El vacío del orgasmo se une al remordimiento
y caes...
Caes...
Gesticulas a tiempo con el goteo
tu vagina se abre como boca de pez

IX

Sigues cayendo
porque has perdido al bebé bé bé é é
Tu incapacidad para comunicarte se deriva del deseo de aprender
a estar sin él
lo peor es que las palabras quieren liberarse quedándose dentro
en ese fondo oscuro que recorres por las noches cuando
Alguien se va
cuando te das cuenta que te quiere
pero se quiere más a sí mismo.
¡Lo amaste tanto, tanto!
¡Ahora no puedes ni debes sufrir!
¡Estás muerta del alma, Juana!

X

La sangre es espesa aunque clara
su olor sale por su boca exhalando un tufo a formol
y han dejado de aplaudir
te miran escrutadoramente
juzgando, señalándote.
¡Esa, ésa es!, dicen con la mirada.
las gasas han dejado de flotar
la banda enmudece
lentamente haces la sonrisa a un lado convirtiéndola en mueca
en una leve mueca de amargura.
Te han descubierto
¿verdá, Juana?
Ya no eres virgen y ese traje de fiesta no te queda
la corona resplandece demasiado chica en tu cabeza
en esa cabecita que piensa engañarlos.
¡Fuiste demasiado lejos con tus ilusiones, Juana!
¡Te están dejando sola!
Sola con tus sueños de grandeza
y el telón está a punto de caer
pero de golpe
con un golpe seco
seco como la hierba que pisaste
que pisaron con sus botas negras
negras como la noche
la noche en que te enterraron
te enterraron con sus cuerpos, erpos, erpos
y contorsionaron tu vientre, entre
entre tus caderas, eras
eras pechos, echos
hechos suero, suero
suero seco, eco
hecho polvo

XI

Cantas una canción de cuna para arrullar al bebé perdido en la
    memoria
en algún drenaje poblado de ratas
¡No hay flores para agraciarlo!
Tu garfio lo acaricia bajo las sombras de la almohada entre
    pucheros y llanto
Ellos decidieron que mandaran a la mierda tu sonrisa
    adolescente, ente ente
porque has sido despojada de la risa, Juana
del placer de descubrir, no lo desconocido
sino lo que no sabes que existe
de la maravilla de la maternidad
del encanto de tu nombre, hombre hombre . . .
Porque nunca fuiste juana, Juana
nunca has sido ni serás juana, Juana:
Eres la hija de don Remigio
la exnovia de Fernando
la violada por . . .
¡Sí, sí, la violada, ada hada!
la loca, oca oca
la que duerme un feto muerto entre sus brazos . . .
Azos azos

XII

Amanece
y la vida no empieza todavía

Lucha Corpi

Márgenes—seis

El olor de tu piel era moreno entonces
y en tus ojos mi cuerpo adivinaba
el negro sortilegio del fuego
aquella noche de orígenes inciertos
en que el rocío sabía a manzana y humo
y tu boca me empujaba mar adentro
hasta las márgenes tempestuosas
de la lluvia y el viento.

Lucha Corpi

Márgenes—nueve

En los ojos que observaron
la tormenta avecinarse
había calles empedradas
y trigales todavía húmedos
por la lluvia de la noche,
un triángulo de sombra
entre dos casas blancas,
un viejo campesino con su violín
envuelto en periódico
en camino a la feria del pueblo.

Me observé en esos ojos
como quien mira en el mar
su imagen fragmentada
por la corriente indómita
y la ve convertirse
en coral
y sombra
y pez
en roca
y mineral fosforecente.

Desde entonces
aprisionado
entre el demiángulo del ojo
y el origen del cantar
como un suicida impenitente
me acecha mi deseo
por sus brazos.

Lucha Corpi

Márgenes—once

A flor de fantasía
tu mirada se extiende
como un tapiz verde y ancho
por mi pensamiento.
Tu boca me sabe a azul
un azul salado y nocturno
y tu cara morena es
un verso de carne
que me sale a los labios.

Mas
al filo del alba
cuando la corporación de la carne
cae en bancarrota
y la orgía civilizada de la luz
comienza
tu recuerdo vuelve a ser
un niño con frío
en la negativa del tiempo.

Barbara Brinson Curiel

Ciudadano de mis sueños

> ¡Feliz quien viva despierto,
> lo que yo he gozado en sueños!"
> *Cancionero de Ripoll*

Tú
ciudadano de mis sueños
esta vida nos plantó
en andenes distintos;

mi tren de amor
me lleva
a un destino cariñoso
lejos del tuyo.

Pero en la siguiente vida
espérame.

Te conoceré
por tus ojos negros como mi sueño,

por la huella empolvada
que te dejé en la mano y en el brazo,

por el hambre que todavía tendrá
mi boca por tu nombre.

Encuéntrame
en un día que sude amarillo
sobre un patio de azulejos—
me estaré quitando las medias.

Reconóceme
por esta ansia en los ojos
que se volverá ancestral,

por la sed imposible
de mis dedos por tu pelo

por el mordizco tierno
que me dejaste
en el hueso del corazón.

Luzma Umpierre

Transcendence

(For Ethel Sager)

He regresado a la ciudad
a soltar a Julia
en mis adentros,
a dormir en la acera este diciembre,
a congelarme los glóbulos de sangre
que salen de mi sexo,
a golpear mis pies
en las parrillas del subway,
a despeinarme, a desgreñarme
el pelo de acá arriba y
el de allá abajo.

He vuelto a la ciudad,
a llenarme los zapatos de espuma,
a rozar mis tetas contra
los cuerpos de la gente en la calle,
a que me toquen las nalgas,
a rezar con aquel hombre
perturbado que me compra una taza de té,
a ver al pueblo hablar de mí en las calles,
a observar, a imaginar, que el mundo se viste
de azul eléctrico o rosa chocante.

He entrado en la ciudad
a abandonar la ropa,
a vestirme de primavera en el invierno,
a declararme prisionera política,
a no bañarme,
a olvidar dónde he dejado mi coche,
a ser conducida por la policía.

Algunos querrían ponerme
al cuello una cadena y pasearme
como a una perra callejera.
Otros querrían llamarme
una mujer loca.

todo por Margarita,
siempre por Margarita,
para poder besar,
uno a uno,
los labios de su amarillo sexo.

Silviana Wood

Sweet Revenge

El Güero de la Tencha never learns.
El otro día, este weekend que pasó,
as a matter of fact,
se emborrachó en la yarda, otra vez,
with the other cementeros,
lost half his paycheck playing poker,
and went home con la cola entre los pies.
Pero cuando la Tencha, ya bien pissed-off con él,
se fue al laundromat con los kids,
el Güero se agarró el cheque del income tax,
hizo forge el nombre de la Tencha,
y lo cambió con el crooked chino de la esquina,
y se fue pa' Nogales
for three days de sinvergüenzadas con la mentada
Rita la Putita, la receptionist del dentista
que usa gas pa' que no te duela, el de la Calle Seis,
la que siempre usa mini-skirts pa' enseñar las nalgas
when she bends over the files,
por eso el Chapo Zepeda va con el dentista every 30 days,
no porque tiene cavities, está molacho el baboso,
pero va pa' verle todo el culo cuando se agacha la Rita
hasta la letter "Z."
Anyway, cuando el Güero le llegó todo crudo y jediondo,
la Tencha ya le había empacado toda la ropa
en three cardboard boxes y las tenía afuera en la curb
pa' que se las llevaran los del garbage.
But Güero didn't care y fue y se acostó
en las sábanas limpias
while Tencha searched the car
and found the dirty pictures
de la Rita la Putita in the glove compartment
y los calzones in the back seat.

Como alacrán encendido, la Tencha
went and got a dirty calcetín
de uno de los buquis,
stuffed it con una bar de jabón Dial,
bath-size,
y le dio por toda la madre al Güero,
que días después went around telling everybody
que la Tencha nomás era muy moody
y que se ponía muy grouchy
especially cuando andaba en su period!
Pero ahora anda el pinchi Güero guarding a la Tencha
como si fuera oro molido, un buried treasure,
porque la Tencha hizo swear revenge
que lo va hacer chivo con el primero
that gets in front of her.
Y el Güero, bien zurrado, dice que that ain't fair.

Así es la vida; qué curada, ¿no?

Ester Hernández   La Virgen de Guadalupe: Defendiendo los Derechos de los Xicanos

Adela Alonso

Virgencita, danos chance

Camila se recarga en el barandal de un puente, contemplando el agua. Deja su mente volar, libre como un pez, frágil como el aire tibio que la envuelve. Contempla el agua y ve unas burbujas; primero redondas y suaves, apenas perceptibles, y luego más grandes, reventándose y formando círculos de agua inquieta. Aparece un cabello negro, sedoso, mojado, lleno de pescaditos verdes y rosas. Parece ser una mujer, sale a la superficie poco a poco y Camila no cree en lo que ven sus ojos. Una mujer bellísima, envuelta en vapor, envuelta en unos mantos rosas, empapados, que dejan ver su cuerpo voluptuoso, sus senos redondos y erguidos. Su boca es una conchita de mar. Pero, ¿quién es esta misteriosa mujer?, se pregunta atónita Camila, mas no atina a hablar ni a alertar a Antonia; Camila la mira embobada. El olor a mar es tan intenso que parecería que esta criatura fuera el mar mismo, su cabello coral y su cuerpo una sirena.

—Camila, te he estado siguiendo, el ser divino emite palabras humanas.
—¿Qué? ¿Yo? pero, ¿quién eres?
—Yo soy la Virgen, la madre de Dios.
—¿Qué dices?, ¿la Madonna? ¿la mera mera?
—Así es Camila, he querido hablar contigo pero te rehusas, no encuentro eco en ti, le dice nada menos que la Virgen.
—Pero cómo, ¿la Virgen?, entonces, ¿sí exististe alguna vez?
—Camila, Camila, siempre tan incrédula, siempre dudando, claro que existo hija.
—No me llames hija, y aun no sé para que me querías ver; es probable que podamos ser amigas pero no me des órdenes no me gusta.
—Camila, pero qué carácter mujer, ¿por qué esa agresividad hacia mí?
—No sé, mmmhmmm, si quieres súbete al puente y vamos a un café, a platicar con calma, son tantas cosas que no sé por cual empezar.

La majestuosa mujer sale por completo del agua y se posa en el puente. Sus pies son casi normales, a excepción de un par de alitas en los talones que la llevan ligerita a donde ella quiera. Camila sigue atónita ante su belleza y el calor que despide, un calor de mar, de eterna primavera. Se sientan a la mesa y Camila pide dos capuchinos.

A Camila le viene a la mente la oración a la Virgen que aprendió cuando era niña y las palabras resuenan en su mente "Ave María purísima, sin pecado concebida, ... sin pecado concebida ..."

—¿En qué piensas Camila?, le pregunta la Madonna.
—Mmmhm ... dime ¿realmente eras virgen cuando tuviste al niño Jesús? Yo la verdad nunca lo creí.
—Ay Camila, le pones tanta atención a los detalles, ¿por qué no ...?
—Pero dime ¿cómo fue todo con José, sentías deseos por él, realmente eras virgen?
—Camila, yo era una mujer como tú, con deseos, gustos, con lo que ahora llaman una "sexualidad" bastante florida. Conocí a José en nuestro pueblo, era mucho mayor que yo y me gustaba tanto, no tienes idea Camila por lo que pasé. José era muy dulce y suave conmigo y una tarde, a las afueras del pueblo, sucedió. Nos amamos debajo de unos olivos horas antes del crepúsculo. Aquello prendió como fuego. Te parecerá extraño oir de las pasiones de los dioses ...
—¿Y te gustó?, preguntó Camila, ahora muy metida en la plática.
—MMMMHMM, José era el hombre más guapo de toda la región, y el más sensual también. Te confesaré que me encantó. Fui tomando experiencia y cada vez lo disfrutaba más. Su piel suave y ardiente junto a la mía, no podía contenerme. Hasta que un día quedé embarazada.
—¡Qué emocionante!, y tu mamá ¿qué dijo?
—En aquellos tiempos las mamás sabían que una se embarazaría y se iría con el hombre, y mi mamá, aunque triste porque me marchaba, me aconsejó, me dió una bolsita con monedas de oro y me regaló el burro para el viaje. Como José era más grande ... pero, un momento, ¿por qué te estoy platicando yo todo esto?, ¿qué estoy diciendo?
—María, perdona que te llame así, es que ya me diste tu confianza y ahora somos amigas, me caes bien. María sonríe y sus ojos brillan con un destello de agua.

—¡Camila, eres imposible!, dice María suspirando y riendo a la vez, ¡incorregible!
Camila sonríe también y mira a los ojos, serenos, suaves, llenos de sabiduría.
—Virgencita, danos chance, a la goma con la virginidad, ¿no? Ya chole con la misma cantaleta del honor, ya estamos hasta el gorro.

Escucha Camila
que en tu tiempo habrá transformación
el paraíso no existe
pero sí una vida de razón
de mayores conquistas
de mejores poderes
Eres como Eva, madre de todas
curiosa
aventurera, los ojos
brillantes
ella fue la primera en conocer
la primera en saber
la primera en elegir
la primera en sentir pasión
Escucha Camila
que en tu tiempo habrá transformación
Como Eva
eres libre
libre
desde hoy tu culpa ha sido lavada con agua
borrada de tu corazón
Sigue a Eva
cabeza caliente
es tu tiempo de transformación

Habiendo dicho ésto la Virgen se inclina hacia Camila y besa su mejilla. Una suave sonrisa se dibuja en su rostro canela y su ropa desaparece en el aire. Camila ve su cuerpo joven, su piel fresca, su vagina mojada, todo lo que uno no ve en las estampitas. Se mira a sí misma también desnuda, ve sus pelitos, sus chichis. La ve. Se ve.

Camila despierta. El sol se filtra suavemente por la ventana que dá al balcón, que dá al canal, que dá a la vida. Ve a Antonia, la dulce Antonia a su lado y sonríe levemente. Camila mira de nuevo a Antonia y se sorprende al ver sus pechos dibujarse contra su delgada camiseta de dormir. Los ha visto miles de veces, desde que eran niñas y no tenía mas que dos circulitos pintados en el pecho, pasando por la época en que Camila no podía dejar de mirar los pechos de Antonia que crecían desmesuradamente, se sentía casi avergonzada por ella pero fascinada al mismo tiempo al ver esos pechos profusos y suaves que crecían por sí mismos, enredaderas después de la lluvia.

Camila recuerda la noche en que se quedó a dormir en casa de Antonia y, mientras Antonia y su hermana dormían, Camila se levantó y se puso un brassier de Antonia que sus pechos más pequeños no alcanzaban a llenar. El usarlo por primera vez le provocó una sensación muy peculiar. Sentir el encaje, el apretado broche en su espalda que comprimía todo su talle, verse reflejada en el espejo bajo una luz azul, de aves nocturnas, se sintió diferente, exaltada. Su curiosidad fue más allá y quiso saber si Antonia dormía con brassier puesto o no y tal vez también quiso sentir sus chichis grandes, temiblemente bellas. Mas Antonia se despertó y Camila, sorprendida en su intento, dijo que estaba tratando de treparse al otro lado de la cama, pues acababa de ir al baño. Después de ese incidente no volvió a preocuparse más de las chichis de Antonia y empezó a aceptar las suyas con un poco más de naturalidad, ya sin intentar esconderlas bajo esas dos trenzas que tejía para cubrirlas, para ignorar su presencia.

Pero esta mañana Camila se siente otra vez sorprendida, como cuando adolescente, al ver las firmes chichis de Antonia, su pezón duro contra la camiseta delgada. Se siente estremecida ante su belleza, su fino y delgado cuerpo, su ropa interior de encajes.

Elvia Alvarado

Don't Be Afraid, Gringo
(Excerpts)

Childhood To Motherhood

I never really had much of a childhood at all. By the time I was 13, I was already on my own. My mother went to live with a man in town. He didn't want to take care of her children, so she left us behind in the village. I wouldn't say she abandoned us; it's just one of those things that happens in life. She kept coming around to see how we were. To this day my mother always comes by my house to see how we're doing.

After I'd been living with my brother for about two years, I started going out with a boy named Samuel. We were both 15 years old and didn't know what we were doing. When we fooled around, I had no idea I'd get pregnant—but I did. In those days, no one ever taught us the facts of life. The adults said that children weren't supposed to learn about such things. So we were left to figure it out on our own.

I remember that the first time I got my period I was terrified. I saw that my vagina was bleeding from the inside. I ran into the woods to take off my panties and look at the blood. I went back home, got a pail from the kitchen, and went to bathe myself. I thought that maybe taking a bath would stop the bleeding. But I just kept bleeding and bleeding.

I was so scared that I stuck some rags in my panties and laid down in the bed. I wrapped the blanket around me, covering myself from head to foot.

My mother came in and asked what was wrong, but I was too ashamed to tell her. I said I had a headache, but she knew I was lying. After I'd been in bed for a few hours, she finally said, "OK. You better tell me what's wrong, or else get out of bed and get back to work."

Don't Be Afraid, Gringo: A Honduran Woman Speaks from the Heart was translated and edited by Medea Benjamin. San Francisco: A Food First Book, The Institute for Food and Development Policy, 1987.

So I told her I was bleeding between my legs. "Don't be scared," she said. "All women get the same thing. It'll last about three days and then go away." When I got the same thing the next month, I wasn't so scared because at least I knew what it was.

Nowadays, the kids learn these things in school. But when I was young nobody told us anything.

Anyway, when my brother found out I was pregnant, he was furious. He said he was going to kill me. I hid in my older sister's house and he went there looking for me. When she told him I wasn't there, he said, "OK. Tell that little slut that I'll be back, and that I'm going to get her with the six bullets I have left in my gun. Because I don't like what she's done to me. I've taken care of her for two years, and look how she's repaid me."

My sister came back crying. She'd never seen my brother so mad. "You better get out of here quick," she said. "The best thing you can do is go to the capital where he won't be able to find you."

Some women have all kinds of problems when they get pregnant—they get nauseous and lose their appetite, or they have headaches, and get real tired. Not me. The only way I ever know I'm pregnant is because I don't get my period. Otherwise I have no other signs.

I worked right up to the last day. When I started getting bad pains, I told the woman I worked for and she took me to the hospital.

I didn't know anything, because it was my first child. But when I felt the labor pains, I just gritted my teeth and clenched my fists until it passed. I didn't cry or anything.

The nurse said, "When you get a really strong pain that doesn't go away fast, push so the baby comes out."

She showed me this cement board they strap you on with your legs wide open—with everything sticking out. She said I should use it when the baby was ready to come out.

I had these pains, and they'd come and go, come and go. Then they started coming faster and faster, until I got this big pain that wouldn't go away. I said to myself, "Ah-ha. This must be what the nurse was talking about."

So I ran over to the board, stuck my legs in the stirrups, and pushed hard. I felt something wet coming out first. And then I felt the baby zooming out, like water rushing out of a bottle when you take the top off. The baby started crying, and one of the other pregnant women ran to tell the nurse.

The nurse came running over, furious. "Why didn't you call me?" she yelled. "You're not supposed to do this on your own." She grabbed the baby, cut his cord, and stuck him in a tub of water.

I don't know why she was so mad. She never told me to call for help, so how was I supposed to know? I just did it by myself. The next day I left the hospital.

When I got pregnant the second time, I didn't bother going to a hospital. I just had the baby at home. I suppose I'm lucky that all my births have been easy; I never had any problems. I've heard the doctors say that when you're pregnant it's good to get exercise so that the child doesn't stick to your stomach. I think that's true, because with all my children I worked and worked until the last minute—washing clothes, ironing, baking bread, grinding corn, making cheese. My stomach would be tremendous. But when it came time to give birth, one big push and whoosh—they'd come out.

■ ■ ■

It was there that I met Alberto and we started living together. I left my children with my mother because she wanted to keep them. But a few months after Alberto and I started living together, the children told me they wanted to come live with us.

I was delighted. But a few days after they arrived, Alberto started fighting with them. He wouldn't give them food. "Let them go back to your mother's house," he told me, "because I'm not about to feed another man's children." What could I do? I had to send them back.

Even while they were living with my mother, they'd come to see me during the day when Alberto wasn't around. I'd give them whatever I had—a tortilla, a piece of bread. I remember one day the oldest boy was sitting at the table eating a tortilla when he heard Alberto come in. He grabbed the tortilla, stuffed it in his shirt, and ran out of the house. I felt awful.

"Look what you've done," I yelled at Alberto. "I can't even give my own children a scrap of food. They're terrified of you. I work my ass off trying to make a few pennies to support my children, and you have no right to stop me from feeding them."

That was when I started having my doubts about living with Alberto. But I was pregnant again, and had nowhere to go.

Alberto and I had three children together. While he worked

out in the fields, I stayed in the house taking care of the children, cleaning, making bread to sell, collecting milk from the landowners to make cheese—anything to earn a few pennies.

Part of the time we were happy together, but Alberto had the same problem my father did—he liked to drink. So while I scraped and saved to buy food for the children, he would spend his money on booze. But at least he didn't hit me like my father hit my mother, and he was good to his own children. That's why I stayed with him.

Marriage Campesino Style

I've heard that there are men and women who make love in all different ways, but we campesinos don't know anything about these different positions. We do it the same all the time—the man gets on the woman and goes up and down, up and down, and that's it. Sometimes the woman feels pleasure and sometimes she doesn't.

We don't have any privacy either, because our houses are usually one big room. So we have to wait until everyone is asleep and then do it very quietly. We just push down our underpants and pull them back up again.

We like to have sex, but we don't let the men see us nude. That's just how we are. As soon as girls are born, their vaginas have to be covered all the time. We never change in front of men; we even take baths with our bras, panties, and slips on. And that's how we sleep, too. Take me and Alberto. We lived together for 18 years and never once did he see me naked.

Not many campesina women use birth control. They just keep having babies, babies, and more babies. I only have six children, which might be a lot in your country but it isn't a lot here. Most campesinas have eight, ten, even twelve children.

I've thought a lot about why we have so many children, and I really don't know why. The men want their wives to have as many children as they can. And most women want a lot of children, too. They think it's only natural.

Part of the reason might be the Catholic church. Most of us are Catholics, and the church tells us that it's natural to have children and that going against nature is going against God.

We campesinas don't have abortions, either. Middle and upper class women have abortions when they don't want the child or when they're afraid of gossip because they're not married. It's illegal, but they have their ways. But the only time campesinas abort is when they're sick and lose the child by accident. We don't abort on purpose; it's not part of our culture.

I never talk about family planning in the campesino meetings. There's one campesino group, ANACH, that gets involved in family planning, because it's a government organization and the government tells it to. They go around telling the campesinos not to have so many children. But the campesinos get mad; they don't like anyone telling them that.

So our group doesn't talk about it. First of all because the campesinos say it's a personal matter, and secondly because there are plenty of other groups that teach about family planning. The church teaches people the rhythm method. The health clinic gives talks about IUDs and pills and all that stuff. And the government has programs on the radio. So we don't have to get involved in those questions.

I personally don't think it's good to have lots of children if you can't maintain them. It breaks my heart to see children suffering because their parents can't afford to feed them. So I think it's good to plan.

My daughters take birth control. I told my daughter Clara that her husband is too poor for her to have another child right now. She has one child, and I think she should wait a few years before having another one—and that's it. Two children are plenty these days.

But to tell you the truth, I don't like my daughters using that birth control, because of all the problems it causes. Those pills do a lot of harm to women here. Maybe they don't affect the gringas so much, because they're more resistant than we are. They're stronger and better fed. But not Honduran women; many of them get sick.

The worst thing we get is cancer. Here in my village six women died recently from vaginal cancer. Before we never had that kind of sickness. At least I'd never heard of it before. But now lots of my friends are dying from it. Some were using pills, others were using IUDs. My sister's in the hospital right now dying of cancer of the uterus.

I once asked a doctor friend of mine, Dr. González, if it's true that birth control causes cancer. He said they haven't been able to prove it yet, but that he was worried about the big increase in women's cancer. All the women I know are scared to death about getting cancer.

Julia Álvarez

The Summer of the Future

She was shaving her legs the day she told us. She called us into the bathroom, my older sister Lydia and me, because we were headed for summer camp and just in case something came up "down there" while we were away. "This is a Kotex, and this is a sanitary belt. It goes around your waist, so and so." She had me all rigged up as her demonstrator, and when she was done, she had me try to put it on myself. Then, she wanted my sister to try it, but Lydia said there was no need for that, she already knew how. That was just like my sister those days she was all grown up and so much better than the rest of us. "Mrs. Know-It-All," my mother scolded her. "Everything is cold turkey to her." She meant "old hat," but her English was still "green behind the ears," and she was always getting the sayings wrong.

"Once a month you'll get it unless you're pregnant or going through the change—"

"What change?" I asked. Mami looked at me, gauging whether I was old enough to be told. "The change when you get too old to have a baby anymore. Any questions?" Mami was nervous and kept nicking her legs with the razor. Little trails of blood were appearing all up and down her legs. "And if any of those American girls try to talk you into Tampax, you say no. N.O. You won't be virgins, and no nice man's going to believe it was just a little tissue rod. You understand?"

My mother always made eye contact and stared us down when she told us what to do. Now her eyes were going everywhere but my face or my older sister's. We understood she didn't really want to be asked anything and so we ushered each other out of that bathroom, afraid she'd cut herself to death before she was finished telling us the facts of life.

Back in the bedroom we shared—my sister called it "the bedroom she had to share with me," Lydia disclosed she had already had her period for several months now. "If you tell, I'll kill you." The look in her eyes was loaded.

I promised. "But why not tell them?" I asked her. "You'd probably get to do a lot more, you know?"

"Are you kidding? Then they really won't let me do anything where there'll be boys involved. Señoritas can't do this, Señoritas can't do that!" She rolled her eyes as if all around there were prison bars. And to top that, she had to share her cell with me, who didn't even see them.

We were going to camp that summer because we weren't going home. My father had been plotting our return back to the island ever since our dictator had been assassinated. Elections had been held last spring, the first in thirty-three years, and nine months ago the new president, who had been a fellow rebel with my father and uncle, had taken office. But then, rumors began circulating: the man was communist. Some military men aided by the Americans took over key military outposts and civil war broke out. The marines landed to protect American lives. Every night my father came home from his office in Spanish Brooklyn, depressed over the latest bad news from "down there." Each time he used the phrase my sister and I would eye each other meaningfully, holding back our laughter, as we remembered how my mother always used that phrase for any point on our bodies bellow the waist. Down there, today, sixty-two had been killed. The Presidential Palace was surrounded. The new president had been forced out of the country. My father did not want to return only to have to leave again in the middle of the night the way we had three years ago under the dictatorship.

"So when are we going back?" My sister and I were homesick and pleaded with him. "Eh, Papi, when?"

"Who can see into the future?" my father shrugged.

"Your father isn't a prophet," my mother agreed. She was liking the life in this country more and more and didn't want to go back. Besides all the tensions of late-night arrests and disappearances down there, she was only "a second grade citizen" down there, as she liked to put it. "I couldn't wear these in public," she'd remark to my sister and me as she slipped on a pair of pants to go out. "If we lived down there, we wouldn't be able to do this," my mother noted when she took us to Fascination once to try the slot machines. "Don't tell your father, okay?"

One night a few weeks before the start of camp my father came home early with the worst news yet. The man who cleaned and tended his office had a short wave radio, and he was almost sure

Marina Gutiérrez   Sisters

he'd heard my uncle's name among those who had been rounded up during a massive purge by the new military government. My father had confirmed the rumor: my uncle had been jailed. My aunt and cousins were under house arrest. My mother wept. We called long distance, and surprisingly, given the other worldly nature of the news we'd just gotten, the maid answered, *Buenas noches.* My mother and father had a stiff, coded conversation with my aunt. Everything was okay, she said too brightly. She was sure my uncle would be released soon. Some misunderstanding . . . Not to forget to have the doctor send his American medicines. Afterwards, we sat around the table in the kitchen, the pull-down lamp just above our heads as if we were under interrogation, my parents trying to decode every word my aunt had said. *Everything was fine* meant, he's not dead yet. *Some misunderstanding* could be the *guardia* hadn't given any reasons for arresting him . . . *The doctor* must be my father, but what *American medicines* could she be asking for? Back and forth they went all during supper as if their solemn, worried voices were shuttles weaving sense out of my aunt's words.

"Maybe she wants you to call up Buchanan, you think?" my mother suggested. Buchanan was an old friend of my family who had a top level job in the State Department, the "connection" that had helped save my father's life by getting him a rush visa into this country. Papi agreed that Mami's guess was brilliant, but his many calls and messages to Mr. Buchanan were never answered. My father was sure he was being given the run around, and the State Department was helping oust the very rebels they had put in power. "We're just guinea pigs to them, Mami," he said bitterly. "Another Bay of Guinea Pigs." It was hard on him to have to accept asylum from the very country which had engineered the situation which forced him into exile.

We went off to camp a few weeks later, my older sister and I, and it near ruined her summer to find out we would be living in the same cabin. My mother had been so nervous about her brother that in filling out the forms, she had mistakenly written my sister's birthday down for us both. The directors thought we were twins and put me in with the Fourteens. Once we were there, one look at my sister and a glance at me, and the mistake was obvious, but there was nothing to be done. I was going to have to bunk with the older girls: Thirteens, my age group, was full. First chance she got, my older sister told everyone she was a year older than I, and I made sure I corrected her, "Eleven months."

My sister should have been secure in what eleven months could do to a body because there was no mistaking she was *at least* eleven months older than I. She had the body of a young woman with her waist curving in like a flower vase and a cleavage where her breasts bunched under her bathing suit just like an Italian movie actress. The camp director looked at her the way he looked at the counselors and the older C.T.A.'s, dwelling on her chest and backside and delicate, shapely ankles. The rest of us campers he looked in the face to see if we were lying or up to some kind of trouble.

My sister had a hard time that summer in camp, our first summer of living among Americans, for even in Queens we were *entre familia*, and not allowed to play with the neighborhood kids. She was homesick for the island and wrote long letters to our cousins and spent hours in the cave of her bottom bunk, playing solitaire, poring over her cards like some sibyl. For a while, she had terrible nightmares and would wake up the whole cabin screaming, and had to sleep in the infirmary. The directors called up my parents, who came up one weekend for a visit, and reassured us that our family was "safely sound," my uncle was still in prison, but the revolution would soon be over and, we'd go back home to live. At breakfast announcements, Mister Holsapple, who was in the habit of catching us up on the world, stopped bringing up "another day of fighting on the little island, homeland of two of our campers." The Rand McNally was folded up to end at the toe of Florida. My sister was sure some horrible truth was being kept from us, but she did calm down, and soon after her nightmares stopped, she moved back into the cabin.

That summer Lydia never quite "passed the mustard." We were our mother's daughters and had picked up many of her malapropisms. She was one of the marginal girls in Fourteens. Her body was much more developed than those of most of our cabinmates, and at early teens, one couldn't go too far either way in the growth spurt without some social ragging. I got some of that for being "a kid," but I had a better sense of humor than my sister, or maybe it was just I could take more put down; also as the summer progressed, my body began to fill out, and there was less of a difference between myself and the slim, exercised bodies of the younger fourteens. But my sister couldn't bear to be teased, and with our accents and mispronunciations, with her "Sophia Loren body" as they called it and my "bird legs," we were often the target of a lot of jokes. I'd shrug my shoulders, make a face, and join in with the laughter even times when my heart was smarting with hurt pride.

In contrast, I, who didn't even belong there, became the popular one, accommodating; running errands, shamelessly, for anyone at any hour; offering my dessert, even when it was chocolate chip cookies, to anyone, picking little crumbs off the picnic tables with a wet index finger. I even got a reputation for seeing into the future and having dreams in which I could tell if someone in our cabin was going to get a letter and what important news it might contain.

It started one night, we were coming back from campfire and I saw clouds massing in the sky in the shape of a ladder. I was feeling euphoric after volunteering to be the rabbit in the counselor skit and bringing down the house with laughter. I was high and happy on woodsmell and the pretty stars overhead. I said, "There's a ladder. Someone's climbing up into heaven tonight." Maybe I meant it mystically at some deeper dream state level, but I think I was just being clever. The next day during breakfast announcements when Mister Holsapple would always get up and tell us what was happening in the larger world, he said he was sorry to have to report that Adlai Stevenson had died the night before. Eyes turned towards me. Little gasps and whispers went around the woodsey dining hall: "The ladder, remember the ladder she saw . . ." To tell the truth, I didn't even know who Adlai Stevenson was. Girls came up to me later with their palms held out like beggars back home. "Tell me if I'm going to get married. Tell me how many kids I'm going to have." I couldn't turn it down, the attention. I took palms in my palm, scowled over the crisscrosses and stitchwork and let myself go into free association as if it were a trance. Soon I had a reputation for being "really psychic." Even Mrs. Holsapple came up to me one night during her cabin visit to the Fourteens, and her bland dull face broke into a coy, gap-toothed smile. "I hear you can see into the future," she drawled. She was from the south and we all imitated her wickedly. I nodded, trying to put on the appropriate serious and sombre face of a true mystic. And then I proceeded to tell her fortune pretty poorly since I had her pregnant with two more kids there was no way on God's earth she could have, on account of she'd had her tubes tied. For several days afterwards, she went into cackles of laughter when she saw me coming. "I'm working on it," she'd howl out, draping a fat, sunburnt arm across Mr. Holsapple's shoulder. I was sure she had me pegged for a phoney, and soon after, I stopped doing handwork, but still there were dreams and signs, there were things to see in the world and I was starting to see them.

One of them was my own body: it was growing and turning a different shape on me, nothing drastic, just emphasis, rounding and arching and swelling where before there had just been flat planes, bones, and black and blues. At first I thought I was gaining weight like everyone else with the starchy food in camp. But my round face hollowed into a woman's in the blurry mirror in the bathroom.

One night we were all sitting around the cabin, and the subject of Tampax came up. Several of the girls used them because they didn't want to fuss with an inconvenient belt and pad, or miss swimming and water skiing five or so days every month, and you couldn't very well put on a suit unless you used Tampax. They talked up some converts, girls who said maybe they should see if they could put them in. The experts offered to give lessons and retrieved their boxes out of their trunks, then led into the bathroom that connected to the main cabin. Lydia stayed in her bunk, playing solitaire, but I, of course, piled into the bathroom, curious to learn as much as I could about the human body the nuns in convent school had only alluded to as the Temple of the Holy Ghost.

The girls who wanted to try the Tampax went into the stalls and shut the doors modestly. They were handed the little packaged rods under the doors and given instructions. They giggled and cried out odd and interesting questions: "but what do I do with the little string?" "What if it goes in and I can't get it out?" "You sure this thing won't break my hymen?" Hymen? I puzzled over their words the way my parents had puzzled over my aunt's coded conversation. Hymen? Did everyone have one? And if so, why hadn't my father, a doctor, told me about hymens? Finally some of girls came out of their stalls rolling their eyes. "I give up! I'll stay with the Middle Ages." Some came out with smirks, and when asked, Had they put one in? They lifted up the empty cigar-shape cover and narrowed their eyes in a sultry look of accomplishment.

The group was getting rowdy with being cooped up in camp for six weeks already. The older girls challenged the younger ones, who had never expressed an interest in changing their gear. It was like an initiation rite in that bathroom, and I was starting to get nervous. First, I was a number one candidate to volunteer since I volunteered for everything else. Second, I had lied: one night while my sister was still sleeping in the infirmary, during one of our after-lights, giggly "lemon squeezes" when everyone was asked the most personal and pointed questions, I had bluffed that, Yeah, I'd gotten my period. I figured if when my sister came back from the infirmary, she caught wind of my lie and tried setting the record straight, I'd come back with, "How do you know? Do you check my panties every day or what?" That would get a laugh.

Some of the bolder girls began to nudge me towards one of the stalls. "Go on, kid! Show us what you're made of!" I shrugged, nah. I'd tried Tampax already and didn't like it. But my refusals only served to whet their appetite to have me comply. I was shoved into one of the stalls and the door was held closed for me. Under the door came the rod. It looked suddenly enormous, too thick to fit anywhere but the edge of my lips as a joke cigar. Then the big jar of vaseline, poked with holes where the girls had dipped their fingers in.

I didn't really know what I was going to do. There was no place to hide that Tampax and I'd already heard our camp counselor lecture that nothing but paper could be flushed down or the toilets would get clogged. I thought of my mother's legs with their little trails of blood and of the lonely future she had foretold for us if we weren't virgins. But at this point in time, it was more important to be accepted by my cabin full of girlfriends from my new country than by some stranger in a suit in the future who wouldn't even let me wear pants in public. I squatted and prepared for the worst.

Suddenly, there were shouts; the group moved off from the vicinity of my stall. I placed my unused Tampax in one of the small brown paper bags and quickly gathered up my pants. I was sure our counselor had entered, and I had literally been left holding the bag. I flushed the toilet to make it sound like I'd been legally using the bathroom, then stepped out and joined the rowdy crowd. They were clustered around the doorway, and as I edged forward, I saw who it was they were taunting and jostling. My sister Lydia was trying to get by to use one of the stalls and whichever way she turned, they blocked her from passing.

"Lydia! Lydia!" They chanted the two syllable name like a cheer. "Lydia, Lydia!" they cried. At first she ignored them, lifting a quivering chin and glancing just above their eyes to avoid confrontation. In her hand, she carried her zippered cosmetics case and as she tried going by the group, she held it to her chest as if it were full of money. Finally, she brushed past their barricade, and over her shoulder as she went by, she hissed at all of them, "Go to hell!"

That was a mistake. They would probably have let her alone if she had kept her mouth shut. "Go to hell," they mimicked her, exaggerating her accent. Then a few of the girls seized her by the shoulders, and when she resisted, they commanded the more passive ones to take her by the legs. They strung her like a hammock between four pairs of girls, holding her by each limb. She kicked and punched, struggling to get free; she yelled curses at them, but she was too proud to plead with them to leave her alone.

I hung back, helpless and frightened. "Let her go, please let her go," I pleaded. But no one was listening. The more my sister struggled and the more she cursed them, the more their fury grew, until they were disposed to hurt her. "Undress her," one of the older girls commanded. "Take her goddamn shirt off," and in no time they had stripped her, though a few of the girls had gotten their stomachs punched and their own breasts kicked in the process.

She stood before us without a stitch of clothes on her woman's body with little girl sobs coming out of her mouth. They had let her go; she was no longer struggling to get away from them; they were the ones embarrassed now—they had intended a prank, perhaps to see two knobby little tits like theirs, not much else—but here was the body we were all growing into, the bodies of our mothers, and some day when we were all old ladies, the bodies of our daughters. Lydia was sobbing now, great wracking sobs, and she was no longer trying to grab at her clothes to hide herself. She stood before us, an accusation. The girls bowed their heads, picked up her clothes, and offered them to her.

It was when I found her panties by the sink where they'd been hurled by one of the girls that I understood why Lydia had risked braving the rabble into the bathroom in the first place. Blurry through my tears, I saw the violet spot on the seat of her pants. It frightened me, for the only blood I'd ever seen came from open wounds. I folded the panties handkerchief size so none of the girls could see what I had seen and handed them to my sister. She did not look at me or at any of the others but quietly accepted her things and slipped into one of the stalls. The door shut. The girls all looked at each other and exited out of the bathroom.

I stood sentinel for a while by that stall. "Lydia," I kept whispering. I tried looking in through the crack at the door, but saw nothing. "Lydia, are you all right?" I asked her. "Lydia, *ábreme la puerta por favor,*" I begged her to open the door. But for a long while there was silence on the other side. I fingered the raw, unplanned wood of the door, feeling the lines and grains, suddenly baffled by what to do, a braille I could not make out. Ahead of us lay a frightening future in a strange, new country. Only its violence was familiar.

Before the summer was out, I caught up with my sister again. One chilly grey day, close to the end of camp, I went into the bathroom and discovered a bright red spot on my panties—no mistaking it. I don't know why I was seized with such panic since I was already well prepared for a period, my belt tucked in its new cellophane package in my trunk, my unused box of Kotex hidden behind my stack of towels so no one could see it unopened there. My older sister had already had her period for several months, and that should have been comforting to me, used as I was to having her precede me into the future and, yes, remind me all the time she was ahead, but also, in a way, trailblaze for me. The world came to me safer through my sister's hands, washed clean with her tears. But that first moment of sighting my own blood, I was afraid. I saw my uncle slump against the prison yard wall, holding his side as his shirt grew red from his bullet wound like a blotter soaking up ink—my only true clairvoyant moment of that summer as I was later to find out.

That night I could not sleep. I had cramps in my stomach and loneliness in my heart, for I didn't dare tell anyone my secret and be discovered as a liar. Late at night, I crept out of my bed and felt my way over to Lydia's bunk. "What's a matter now?" she grumbled. That was her way always of asking me what I wanted, linking it to the last request, a long chain of my indebtness to her and her bondage to me. When I didn't answer, she lifted her blanket and let out a long, self-sacrificing sigh. "Come on. It's cold out there!" She spoke in English, for we were quite the Americans by the end of the summer and felt as comfortable in one language as the other. I crawled in beside her. "I got my period," I confessed to her.

"I hope you put that belt on right; I don't want my sheets all dirtied," she scolded, but then on a nicer note, since she must have felt bad to have greeted my coming of age with a comment our mother might have made, she added, "We're in for it now. Señoritas can't do this, Señoritas can't do that . . . Misery makes strange bedfellows, as Mami would say." She let out chuckles that were like the muffled snores that came a little later on from her side of the bed.

I lay beside her a long time after she had fallen asleep, listening in the dark to her breathing and that of the campers curled up in their different bunks. Above us my sister's bunkmate shifted sides in her sleep and for a moment the bed creaked like the cabin was a great boat set adrift. I felt a sharp pang on my side and briefly tried to guess what organ was around those parts that might be breaking down. For suddenly, I knew I was old enough to have a baby, old enough for anything. To die even like my uncle and my mother and my father and my sister, each in their own time. I reached out my two hands, lined with future I no longer wanted to know, and held on to my sister. "Go to sleep," she mumbled in her sleep.

Gloria Anzaldúa

La historia de una marimacho

Para que le cuento, en aquel tiempo era mal visto que una mujer quisiera a otra. Cásate conmigo, le rogaba. Pero, ¿cómo me voy a casar contigo, mujer?, me decía cuando andaba de buenas y se reía. Me gustaba mucho esa muchacha. ¿Qué le va una a hacer cuando se le mete el amor hasta el corazón? Entregarse a esa llama. Cortando calles como un perro la espiaba, como un perro poco a poco engentándome más con ella.

Al principio sentí tanta vergüenza cuando sus nalgas me alborotaban. Era chaparrita, me llegaba aquí, al hombro. Tenía unas manos delgaditas, exquisitas, no gruesas como las mías. 'Taba bien buena. Siempre traía una mascada en el pescuezo.

La esperaba. Y cuando ella salía de la casa la acompañaba. Tan bien que nos veíamos brazo en brazo, yo en mi ropa de hombre y ella en su falda de olanes y blusa blanca con encaje amarillo. Yo era muy atrevida y ella muy avergonzada cuando la tocaba. A veces la ofendía con mis declaraciones y algo en mis ojos la asustaba. Un día no me pude aguantar y le besé la boca. La vieja Marta nos vio. Me tullí.

"Ay dios mío, muchachas ¿qué están haciendo allí en lo oscuro?" dijo la vieja, persignándose. "Ave María purísima." Y que se echa a correr como si hubiera visto al demonio. Estábamos pegadas, encerradas en las sombras de su patio, un patio cercado de macetas y ladrillo. "Ya déjame," me murmuró ella en el oído. "La vieja va a chismear."

"A mí no me importa. Lo que sí me vale es que cuando sales a la calle los pelados te tiran unos chiflidos. Los desgraciados quieren meter mano," le dije. Me entraba una rabia al ver a los hombres chuleándola. Ella era mía. Gracias a dios que ella no era como muchas mujeres, mansas y mensas. Como quiera, me encelaba. ¿Qué diablos andábamos haciendo como las mendigas a las escondidas?

Un atardecer oí a su papá gritándole, "No 'tés jodiendo. Te

digo que no vas a salir con ella. ¿Qué te estás creyendo? ¿Qué puedes hacer lo que te de la gana? Tú tienes la culpa que esa marimacho esté empelotada contigo. Y tú, alcahuete," oí que el padre le dijo a Juan, "a la mejor tú también eres uno de los otros. Qué te andas metiendo en las naguas de las viejas, tú." Ví que se asomó por la ventana y al divisarme levantó su puño. "Esa sí es jota de a de veras, no quiero que tengas nada que ver con ella. ¿Me entiendes?", le gritó su papá. "Si agarras ese camino te mato. Lo juro que te mato." Había sido mi buen amigo Juan y no la vieja Marta quien me echó de cabeza. Ah, qué mala suerte me hice en confiar en él.

Pasaron unos días. Ví que no la dejaba salir de la casa. Una tarde me arrimé a su corredor. Su papá abrió la puerta. "¿Qué quieres?" me preguntó.

"Le vine a pedir a usted la mano de su hija," le dije.

"Que pendejadas se te ocurren," me dijo, echándose a reír a carcajadas. "Búscate un muchacho bueno y deja de meter mano adonde no te pertenece."

"A mi ningún pelado me ha metido mano, ni me la va a meter. Con una mirada que les dé se van muy escurriditos con la cola entre el culo," le contesté.

"Pos que pueden hacer dos mujeres. Pa' eso se necesitan huevos, ja, ja, ja."

Me quedé con un coraje que me mareaba y un corazón vacío. Toda la noche se jugaban en mis párpados insurgentes imágenes. Me la va a pagar ese hombre, juré.

Cuando amaneció me fui a la calle a espiarla. A veces la divisaba por la ventana. Un atardecer cuando ví que su papá salía, me arranqué pa'l patio. No sé que me entró, me tragué el grano que se me había atorado en la garganta y le dije, "Quiero que huyas conmigo." Ella me vio con esos ojones que me caían tan bien y luego agachó la cabeza. Se había atravesado en mi vereda y ahora no la iba soltar huevos o no huevos. "No te me cabrées," le rogué pero ella no levantó la cabeza.

"¿Qué vida podemos tener?" me dijo al fin. "Pa' ti la vida es tu lucha y eso es tu herencia. Pero no pa' mí. Yo soy muy miedosa, tú lo sabes."

"¿Me quieres o no me quieres? Quiero saber de una vez," le dije pescándola de los brazos.

"Tú sabes muy bien que te quiero, ésa no es la cuestión. ¿Qué vamos hacer dos mujeres, sin dinero, sin amigos, sin tierra? Nadie

nos va a recoger, somos una cochinada. Yo sé que mi padre nos buscará hasta que nos halle."
"Me voy," le dije.
"¿Pa' dónde vas?"
"Rumbo a lo triste," dije yo. Un grito sin boca me acompañó por el camino. "Una vez más virgencita, quisiera verla," le recé. Eché mis garras en un costal y ensillé el caballo y la yegua. Puse pie en el estribo y le metí las espuelas. Cuando llegué a su ventana rasguñé la tela. "Vine a despedirme. Ya me voy para otras tierras. ¿Tú qué intentas?" le dije en voz baja.
"Intento ser libre, me dijo."
"Andale pues, niña linda."
"Aquí esta mi morral, vámonos, a volar la jaula."
La monté en la yegua alazana. Ella se persignó. En esa noche de luna, sin pedirle su bendición, dejó a su padre, dejó a su casa.

Jalamos pa'l norte rumbo a quién sabe dónde, atravesando maizales hasta que entramos al mesquital. Amanecimos en Los Ebanos. Ella se quedó con los animales en las afueras del ranchito. Dejé los caballos ensillados pero les desapreté los cinchos. Alcé mi cabello y lo tapé con mi sombrero tejano. Me fui a comprar provisiones: harina, arroz, manteca, frijol y un sombrero pa' que no se me asoleara.

Al tercer día desveladas y hambrientas vimos el amanecer cien millas al norte. Allí en la boca de un río su pelo largo brillaba. Le bajé los calzones y besé el lunar descolorido que tenía en una nalga. Allí en donde las olas se quiebran me apretó los pechos. Ese día probamos de todo.

Me volví a acostar a su lado. En la noche parecía que oía la voz de su papá: A esa jija de la chingada, le voy a dar unos chingazos.

A mí, mi gente no me buscará. Después que murió mi madre, mi hermano me comenzó a manosear. Cuando no me dejé me corrió de la casa. A mí no me manda nadie.

Allí en la boca del río pasamos una temporada. Una mañana cuando abrió los ojos le pregunté que si quería volver a su padre. "Nuestra vida no va ser fácil."

Se me medio enojó. "¿Pos qué tienes tú?" me preguntó. "La vida amenaza a todos, rico o pobre, hombre o mujer."

"Sí, pero amenaza más a la mujer, y más todavía a las mujeres como nosotras," le dije. Me sentía extraña, presentía lo malo.

"Vamos," me dijo, "a subir a donde nace el río." Mes tras mes caminamos por tierras ajenas y cuando daba con trabajo nos quedábamos unos cuantos días o semanas. No sé cómo la gente siempre se daba cuenta que no era hombre. Pero dándose cuenta malas caras nos hacían y nos daban sus espaldas. Al completar un año de 'casadas' llegamos al cerro Altorojo. Allí en su lomo fundimos nuestra vida.

"De aquí no me mueven viva. Jamás comeré los polvos del camino," le dije. Por tres años cultivamos la tierra, criando chivos y borregos. Un día llegué de la pasta a tropezarme con su papá en la cocina. Ella estaba tirada en el suelo. De su cara le escurrían lágrimas y sangre. Levantó la cara. Sus ojos me suplicaban. Le quería romper la cara al desgraciado pero me detuve, comiéndome el coraje.

Levantándose del suelo, a su papá ella le dijo, "No, no me arrepiento. No cambiaré por oro o plata ni un segundo de mi vida con ella."

"¿Pero qué vida es ésta, hijita?"

"Nuestro cariño es tan fuerte, papi, como el tuyo pa' mamá. Ningún amor es corriente, ni el de una mujer pa' otra."

"Mire viejo, por el amor de su hija detengo mi mano. Pero viejo, óigame bien, a mi mujer nadie le alza la mano. Un castigo requiero por la paliza que le dio."

En la mano todavía traía el machete. Como mazorcas desboqué los dedos de la mano que le había pegado y luego destronqué su oreja. Dedos y oreja cayeron al suelo como animalitos muertos. El no les quitaba la vista.

Seguro que le pegó compasión. No sé si fue el susto que le dí, pero desde ese día comenzó a cambiar sus modos. Se me hace que el viejo tenía miedo de morirse lejos de su única hija.

Le hice un cuartito detrás de la cocina y cuando se sanó de la mano comenzó a trabajar a mi lado. Parecía indio con su paño doblado alrededor de la cabeza tapando el agüjero que más antes fue su oreja.

Fue entonces que los muchachos le pusieron otro verso al corrido:

La mujermacho alzó su machete,
Allá en San Juan Puñacuato.
Los dedos de don Rafo saltaron
Y se le escurrió su coraje.

De la gente se oye decir
Que ya un hombre no vale nada
y hasta los huevos le estorban
a los machos de San Juan Puñacuato.

Denise Chávez

from *The Face of an Angel*
(a novel in progress)

Mama Lupita wanted one of her grandchildren to become a nun. Priests in the family are a dime a dozen. Everyone knows they are either jotos or maricones or lusty goats in search of skirts. What this family needs is a nun. Women's prayers, anyone knows, are more powerful. Any man can give up sex for four years, especially if they get them before they know what to do with that thing between their skirts. Cassocks that's what they call them. After that, you know what happens. When a woman gives up sex, it's final. Try and sneak sex on a woman, see what happens. Nine months later there's everlasting hell to pay. No m'ija, you are the one, Soveida. You are going to be a nun, someday, one day, may I live to see it, and if I don't, you'll never rest m'ija till it's done or you're done or I'm done. One way or another. One time or another. Everyone woman wishes she could become a nun. You don't know what I mean yet, m'ija, may the Blessed Mother spare you a drunken man late at night smelling of chicharrones and tequila, worse yet of frijoles and beer, worse yet a man in the middle of the afternoon in August when you're roasting chile and he comes in from the farm, smelling of sweat and dirt and carrying on, as if it wasn't hot enough already. I want to spare you this, m'ija, listen to me. Think about it. You like to read. Nuns read all the time and no one interrupts them. They can be quiet and have no one belch out loud and scratch themselves or make pedos you know, on the way to the you know what, the excusado. A word like that. It sounds like an excuse. That's what sex is, but in a different way. And once in the excusado, Dios mío de la vida, the noises and later the smell. I keep matches in there but your grandfather Profy, he don't use them. Men can't be trained. They're wild bulls or changos, monkeys, I don't know which. And that's not all. They shed. I could never keep a clean tub.

I want to spare you the details. Think about the divine service. I know what Father Escondido thinks marriage is, m'ija, just let him take three rounds with my viejo, let's see what he says. So, think about it. I mean, becoming a nun. Your mother's childhood friend, Estella Fuentes became a nun. She's now Sister Mary Margaret Marie of the Holy Magdalenes. She don't have no wrinkles. Her face smooth like a baby's nalgas. Look at Dolores' eyes. A road map. Tejas. Luardo did it to her, and he's my son. With him, priesthood was out of the question from the beginning. He was always pulling on his cosita; there was no way he was ever to be consecrated. Ni lo mande Dios! It's as if some children have an invisible sign on their foreheads: Priest. Married Man. Pendejo. No, I knew. The man was oversexed from the day he was born, no way he could have ever been ordained. The thing would have stuck out through his skirts. Him, he should have been, you know, right then and there, but he was my first born, for all the shame it brought this family, all the trouble it caused your Mama, not to mention all the others . . . En el nombre del padre, del hijo, y del espíritu santo . . . He may be your Daddy, but he's half man, half goat. What half the goat you'll have to guess. Testudo como chivo, that's what I say, he thought with his costia, not his head. Look at your Mama. That road map near her eyes. California. All on account of you can imagine. She didn't have no chance. It had a will of its own. Como Chile Colorado. Think about it, m'ija, think about the Divine Service. You like to read.

■   ■   ■

Lawrence Larry Lencho Lar L. Larragoite was the owner and sole proprietor of El Farol Restaurant and Bar, specializing in Mexican food and steaks. The Restaurant had been handed over to him, lock, stock and barrel by his mother, Consuelo "Connie" Larragoite La Point Bexler, after she had run it for many years, and after Larry had almost received his B.A. degree in Business. He was nine hours short. He's gone back east to Vermont because his mother's brother, Milo Larragoite, or as Milo was known there, Mr. Laragoitey, lived there, and because secretly, his mother Connie didn't want him to marry a Mexican. She thought if he got away he'd meet someone nice, someone Anglo. Connie's first marriage had been with a Mexicano, Eddie Larragoite, Larry's dad, but he had left her for countless other women, and she couldn't take it anymore. One day Connie just walked out with Larry and never went back. The last anyone had heard of Eddie L. was that he had moved to California, had a new family and had stopped drinking, as well as carrying on with other women.

Connie thought if Larry got away far away from the state he'd meet someone nice. And that meant someone ANGLO. To her there were two main races: ANGLO and Mexican. She was a MEXICAN mexican and Eddie had been a mexican mexican. The combination could never work.

She knew from experience the hell she was saving her son from. Now it was a lot different with women, but the badness was in the blood and it was in the genes. Connie wanted her grandchildren to be different. She wanted them, all little girls she hoped, to find men who would appreciate them, put them on a pedestal, the way Willie and Herman had done for her.

Not that she hadn't loved Eddie, dadgum she loved that man, even though he had jungle rotty feet from the war #2 and knew what it was to love a man with athlete's feet. The man was the best lover she'd ever had, ever would have, but he just wasn't dependable. With a small child and countless bills, it was either Eddie had to go or her sex life. She had really tried to work it out, that's how the restaurant was born, but if he wasn't dipping his fingers into the cash box he was monkey-ing around with the hostesses. It was either Eddie or her son's future. Eddie has had his past, present and what future was there for an out and out in and out. Larry, on the other hand, was her son first born, only born.

To this day she couldn't eat red chile. The night before Larry was born she'd eaten a plate of red enchiladas Dora la cocinera had fixed for her at El Farol. She was still up and around then and she still believed that was what brought the labor on. And what a labor it was! Later that next day the hospital staff was till cleaning up chile from the floor. Connie couldn't look at red chile now without thinking of Larry and her decision, then and there to tie her tubes. No man nowhere ever was going to cause her that especially one she loved, red chile or not! I love my baby but I swear to you Lady Blessed Mother Queen of Angels on my mother's grave it hurt like hell and don't you ever tell me that the pain was worth it. I love my baby but goddamn no way in hell, forgive me little mother, any man ever, especially one I love, gonna do that to me ever again, may I burn in everlasting hell full of unfaithful lying through their teeth men no man ever gonna do that to me.

Eddie Larragoite just wasn't husband material.

Lover material, maybe, but not husband and father material. Although Connie heard later that Eddie had had three daughters all of whom looked like him and that he had turned out all right. Bastard.

Connie had fared better with husband #2 and #3, Willie LaPoint, and Herman Bexler. Each of them rich Anglos who knew how to treat a woman. And yet, there was that nagging worm in her soul whose name was Eddie Larragoite. If she closed her eyes she could still smell that acrid sweet wave of yellow crusty putrefaction that the man she still loved somewhere called his feet. They were the feet of an old miner, a gone to seed sportsman, a prisoner of war. They were the feet of Eddie Larragoite. The only man she'd ever loved. The only man she swore she never wanted to grow old with. The only man who gave her his seed, a seed she allowed to remain.

Claudia Colindres

A Letter To My Mother

This is a letter you may never read; because it may hurt you. I wish I could tell how much I admire your strength, your ever lasting quality of always giving yourself to my sisters, my father and all your relatives. You seem so content to always care for others, but how about yourself?

For me mom, the story is different. I am engaged in "intellectual thought" that many times makes me feel like a man; many times I feel unsensitive, competitive and uncaring. I hate this feeling, because I know how sweet you are. Are you sweet and caring because you never finished grade school? I feel as if all this knowledge, all the papers I have written, puts a distance between you and me, and still I feel very much like your daughter. The impossibility of changing myself kills me. I know that I will become like you, whenever I reach your age, I know that physically I look like you. Your friends always say we look alike, and you in turn look like my grandmother, your mother. Well, will I be like you? I am afraid that this college education I have struggled so much to achieve will cause irreparable changes in my perceptions of womanhood. These new perceptions of womanhood are at odds with our traditions, and I am afraid that these differences in the way we express our femaleness may cause friction between you and me. I don't want to betray your teachings, but I feel that if I follow the female traditions of our culture, I will perpetuate sexism, by transmitting those notions of womanhood to my future sons and daughters. I wonder if I will I be as sweet as you are, or will I be an antiseptic woman, with a career and professional friends? If I become like you, will I ignore all I have learned about patriarchy? Will I deny the monetary value of my household toiling, once I get married? Will I serve my husband's needs without expecting the same of him towards me? Will my marriage work if I step out of the traditional wife role you taught me?

Mother, at this point in my life, I wonder if marriage could exist without the subjugation of the female. I sense, that although legally it is a contract with equal responsibilities, in practice I have seen how you always gave in. You were the only one that carried all the blame, as if it was a marriage where you were the only one that signed the papers and made the promises. The whole society looked at you and thought that you were not good enough to keep a man. They thought that perhaps your cooking skills needed some improvement, or that you needed to lose a couple of pounds. Nobody ever condemns the man, it is always the wife, the one who needs to learn how to "trap" a man, even when the contract of marriage has been signed by the man and the woman. In the university I have learned the definition of a contract, and when I get married it will be a contract. That is, my husband will have equal blame if the marriage does not work out. Mom, I am not willing to always be the one giving in and letting my needs be taken care of last. I am afraid of breaking the traditions of marriage in our culture. As a result, I hope you won't remind me of the traditional ways, or that you don't condemn the way I will behave towards my husband. Most likely you will be disappointed because I won't follow your example. I won't cook all the time, I won't do the dishes or the laundry all the time. My husband will help me; the chores will be distributed equally and the decisions will be joint decisions. Mother, if I do all these, I will betray your teachings. You always cooked dinner, you always cleaned up the kitchen, did our laundry and my father never helped you. Please do not think I am criticizing your marriage with dad. It is just that I see you wear out, get wrinkles, your hair is grey and my father looks fine. He has no grey hair, and he has time to exercise. I think that your toiling with the children, the dogs, and the chores absorbed your youth, beauty and character, and I don't want to look old and be worn out at age forty-two. Mother, I have chosen the path of self-determination and I hope you understand this once I establish my own household.

Mom, when I sit in my class and we discuss *machismo* I think about you. You were raised in a family that strongly emphasized the rights of the male. My grandfather never allowed you to go to college, because he felt you were weak, *una mujer*. He argued that if in college somebody played a joke on you he would have to defend your honor. Grandpa explained to you how problematic it would be for him to leave his office in order to defend you, but he never taught you to defend yourself or explained to you the value of an education. Since Grandpa never taught you how to defend yourself in a man's world, he either defended you, which he did not want to do, or you stayed home and learned how to mop the floors. Never did he give you the option of defending yourself, because of your gender.

You internalized the weakness they preached to you. You believed Grandpa and my uncles when they said people would play jokes on you. You believed them when they lectured you about how a real lady's honor is protected by her father and her brothers. They never told you to pull it off by yourself, they did not want you to. You still believe you are stupid and weak. Mother you are not. It really hurts me, when you say you are not intelligent, but that you have experience. Mother you have experience, but only because you are intelligent can you apply it. I get so upset in class when we talk about patriarchy, it is so frustrating to know that you are a product of it. Mother if I could change you, would you still be as sweet?

I think you are sweet because you always took care of others like myself, first, and then you took care of yourself. I remember when times were bad, you would feed and clothe us first, and if there were any leftovers or extra cash then you would eat or buy yourself the needed dress or shoes. Mother, you always left your needs for last. I now realize that it was to my advantage, as your child, but as a woman I know it was because you had no other avenues to explore but that of motherhood. Please do not think I despise motherhood, on the contrary I think it is a hard and unsafe task and I admire women like you, who with limited resources, bring up four or five children in the most loving ways. Your sweetness was imposed on you, being a woman it is the only way you could be. Sweetness was your only defense and tool to survive. It is the only thing your parents taught you. They did not enhance your strength of character, nor the aggressiveness you sometimes show. They curtailed these traits and forced you into a subservient, conformist woman; the dream wife for all your brother's friends! You did not have the options that I have now, and I resent myself, because I was one of the beneficiaries of your womanhood. I resent myself, not only because I benefited from your self denial, but also because I will never be able to make it up to you, to give you all the options your parents, your brothers and society at large denied you.

Don't take me wrong, I really admire you, and believe me I am proud of being of your blood. I just wish I could share with you my youth and strength, and undo all the years of sexism you have experienced, so as to show you my ways of womanhood. Going to college has given me the options and tools to define myself, to be myself. Education goes beyond mere monetary opportunities, to me that is the last thing I think about. These four years of college have taught me to be real; to believe in myself. Sadly, often times I feel as if when a woman goes to college, she has to become part "male." It is almost impossible to finish college with your sexual identity intact. If you saw the competition, and the treatment we receive! Not only are we sexual prey to most of the men, but we also have to become assertive and competitive. Many times, if you are a woman, you have to prove yourself to everyone, nobody believes you until you prove yourself. In the classroom, for example, I have said many things and nobody listened, but when a man rephrases what I said, he gets all the attention and credit. Mamá, you know how it is in our culture, women are not supposed to be outspoken! Mother, if I change, in order to survive, will you still accept me as a woman, as your daughter? I promise you I will try to be sweet, to be understanding, to be caring, and nurturing, just as you are. In this society women have to become "masculine" to survive—at least survival strategies are classified as masculine.

In college, I have learned to be number one, I am the first priority to myself, and school is the second one. I am selfish and career oriented, and this act of putting myself and my goals first is in conflict with your ways Mother. I am split, because I want to follow your example, I respect you, I admire you, but at the same time school has made me so self-oriented that I realize I have learned to behave as my father does. I want to be like you and at the same time I don't. I want to care for my children as you took care of me, but I don't want to sacrifice myself as you did. I want to go to Church, but I don't want the audience to be all female. Mother, I want a world where men and women are equal, where women can decide their own futures without having to worry about going to a moral hell. I wish men changed their attitudes towards parenting, marriage and religion so as to eliminate all the double standards that exist in our culture. I realize I will never see the world as you do, so I will never be able to be like you, a saint. No, mother, they won't change or they haven't so the other way is for women to demand equality. By doing this, they are using "male" strategies and learning to survive as "men," never as "women." When I say to you that I am learning to be a "man," I really mean it, because I am learning to put myself first. Putting myself first, is awfully hard, because in my brain I have it engrained that women should be like the Virgin Mary. Being docile like Mary is impossible when you have to compete for grades.

The funny thing is that my white friends cannot conceive of, nor understand when I tell them about the "masculinization" process we go through when we attend college. They were brought up differently, and for them being self-oriented is second nature. I met the mother of one of my Anglo friends; Mom that is the key difference between them and I. My Anglo friends' mothers, sometimes even grandmothers, went to college and as a result learned to behave like "men." It seems to me that since in the Anglo (European-American) culture the Catholic Church is not the predominant religious institution, women believe in the right of self-improvement. They do not only believe in it, but they struggle for it, whereas in our Latin American culture if a woman demands or speaks out for her rights she immediately is branded, labeled. My friends don't have submissive mothers. This society does not demand submissive mothers, although sexism is still alive and well. The difference is that white women seem so much freer in their actions, and I think this difference is because their culture is not filled with Catholic overtones, and because women have been allowed into higher education. If you saw the mother of a friend I met—she treated her children as equals. She chose to have children and she chose when to have them. She took care of them when they were small, but she was always herself, never "The Mother" or "The Wife" but "Fulanita". She never accepted to become one of those generic symbols that society assigns to women, she had the option to be different. Her parents sent her to college, and their neighbors never censured them. I don't know if you always wanted to be "The Mother" or "The Wife," but I wonder if you had had a choice, would you be my mother?

I know that for you it was different, the circumstances were out of your control. Had you attended college, your prestige and reputation as a woman would have been tainted, one of the first insults would be Machona. My Anglo friends' mothers lack the abnegation you have. I don't condemn your abnegation, as I said earlier, as your child I benefited from it, but I wonder how much choice you had in choosing your ways. I think that only Latinas and perhaps Chinese women would understand what I am talking about when I say that school teaches us how to deny our traditional womanhood. My white classmates have college-educated, "masculine" mothers and cannot understand me. I say this because when we talk about growing up they say that their mothers always placed themselves, and their needs first.

Mother please do not ask me to keep inside me my feelings of anger and frustration when I see you degrade yourself because you are a woman. For example, when my father needs advice, and you don't offer your advice because you know that he won't listen, it upsets me. It upsets me because you don't give validity to your ideas, and everybody should, including you. Mom, being a woman is more than what my grandfather taught you. It is true that part of being a woman is bearing and rearing children, making tortillas, smelling good, being quiet, being sweet, obeying, praying, going to church and an endless list of tasks assigned to us by men to please men. Being a woman also includes many other things, and usually you have not engaged in these other activities because of your lack of time and money. I refer to writing, singing, laughing, expressing your feelings in an open way, saying what you think without feeling awkward. I also talk about getting to know your body better, accepting your femaleness not as a tool to attract a nice looking boy, but for yourself. And mom reading! How happy I would be the day I see you pick up a book and read it. Reading is not a priviledge for men only, I read and all of my sisters read, you should read too. Being a woman is an integration of all these things, a woman is not complete until she can accept her feelings and herself wholly. I know that to you, being deeply Catholic, this may sound like gibberish. I wish I could convince you that the Catholic Church and almost all religions are sexist. Religion, and sadly, religious figures such as La Virgen de Guadalupe, have been used by priests (100% male) to seduce and manipulate the female psyche. I will respect your religion, I just wish we could talk about it without you thinking I am being blasphemous or as you would say *indigna*.

Mother, I am not trying to change you. You are a wonderful person. I learned this when I was planning to leave home to come to Berkeley. It was in my senior year of high school that I saw your true colors. You were my ally, and you stood by me, when my father tried to do to me what your father did you, he was trying to keep me home, because I am a woman, *una mujer*. It was great to see you talk to him, scream to him that I had the right to pursue an education. It was invigorating! You were strong and powerful. You urged me to go away and continue my education, even when you knew that I am a woman and therefore in your eyes also *mujer*.

You know, being away in time and space is hard because I miss sharing with you. Still, mother, as I said before I always think of you, especially when I am enjoying myself, my freedom. I wish you could be with me and learn with me. I wish I could bring you up, as I grow up. I also think of you when we talk about family structure, familism, and especially motherhood. I feel happy that I can think of you, and incorporate whatever experiences we shared, as mother and daughter, into my "intellectual thought and development". Mother I wish one day we could talk about the situation in which I find myself—that of constantly trying to redefine my womanhood according to society at large, our culture, all the knowledge I have acquired, and your personal example. This situation is a challenge for me, I am trying to be a woman in a "man's" universe. I hope that once I am out of school we can share, without fear of hurting each other, what you feel about your womanhood, and what I feel about mine, and together analyze the difference, without you thinking that I am crazy, or an atheist, or amoral, or weird, or a "man". I hope that this college education never stops our flow of communication and understanding. I hope I never become antiseptic like some of the women I have seen around. I hope I can remain as sweet as you have always been, without having to compromise my goals or my needs as a human, as a woman. The only reason I want to be like you is that you are good person, to me a wonderful mother. I don't want these years of schooling to engrain in me greed, money, success, fame and all those things most college educated people struggle for, I want to be as good and caring as you are Mom.

And if dad reads this letter, he will also be hurt for the way I portray him but tell him that I know that he has been a victim of sexism as much as you have, because he himself never had the option of defying all his male friends' code of behavior. Had he been a feminist, boy, he would had been called beautiful names!

Erlinda Gonzáles-Berry

Conversaciones con Sergio
(Excerpts from *Paletitas de guayaba*)

¿Cuándo fue que nos vimos? ¿Apenas cuatro días? No lo creo. Sabes que cuando paso un día sin verte, te extraño tanto que me quiero morir. ¿Verdad que apenas hace cuatro días? A mí se me hizo más. Pero sabes que también me gusta cuando no nos vemos por algún tiempo porque siempre son mucho más intensos mis orgasmos después. No se, duran más. Hoy por ejemplo, fue increíble, como una torrente de ola tras ola de espasmos eléctricos. Creí que nunca iba a terminar. ¿Te imaginas lo que sería quedarse una atascada en un orgasmo perpetuo? Sería algo así como las personas que no pueden dejar de estornudar, placer y agonía. En términos puramente biológicos, el estornudar es semejante al orgasmo, ¿no te parece? A mí, por ejemplo, me encanta estornudar. Siento gran satisfacción y placer al hacerlo.

Sabes que el primero, digo el primer orgasmo, siempre es fantástico. Claro, porque es el descargo de una tremenda acumulación de energía pero de ninguna manera se le acerca ni en intensidad ni en satisfacción al segundo o al tercero. No sé cómo explicarlo, pero estos parecen originarse en un sitio mucho más profundo que el primero, especialmente si vienen bien seguiditos. A veces siento que brotan del mero centro de mi ser físico y espiritual. No te rías. No sé cómo explicarlo. La verdad es que es imposible describir la sensación pero, *sans doute*, vale la pena, aunque a veces cueste tanto trabajo lograrlo. Dime la verdad, ¿no te dan celitos que yo pueda tener un montón de orgasmos sin esperar, digo, sin recuperarme del primero? La otra noche estábamos hablando Toña, Lupe, Isaura y yo, y decidimos que el patriarcado se debe al orgasmo múltiple del género femenino. Estoy hablando en serio. Mira, si la hembra es capaz de tener múltiples orgasmos, quién le va a impedir que se largue con otros mientras el primero se recupera. Claro después habría un lío con quién es el padre—pero eso ya es otra cosa. Así que tú lo ves más bien como asunto de la herencia de la propiedad privada. Bueno, eso ya lo sé, pero de ninguna manera disminuye la posibilidad de que exista alguna relación entre la posición social (*not to mention* la posición supina en el acto conyugal) de la mujer y su propensidad al orgasmo múltiple. Mira, creo que cuando el hombre, Adán o quien fuese, se dió cuenta de esta dádiva femenina, se percató de lo difícil que sería controlar a su Evita querida. (A lo mejor sí fue Segusmundito como dices, pero me imagino que ya andaba por allí esta información en los tiempos de Adán). Pucha, hasta con la serpiente era capaz de escabullirse la malagradecida. Así que ¿qué hacer? Según mi interpretación, puramente personal, ¿entiendes? se ofrecían dos soluciones. Una, negarle a la mujer esos múltiples orgasmos, haciéndole creer que el único orgasmo genuino era el orgasmo inducto por el órgano masculino inyectado en el receptáculo femenino. Ahora bien, si no quedaba satisfecha, y puesto que él tenía que recuperarse, ¿cómo permitir métodos heterodoxos (deditos, lenguitas, etc.)? Ni modo, porque esto le daría a ella la idea absurda que su placer no dependía de *you know what*... el instrumento sagrado. Seguía que cualquier mujer insatisfecha con el único orgasmo, claro, vía el coito, *non erat mulierum integram*. Ahora bien, como siempre existía la posibilidad de que hubiera por allí rebeldes, digamos, chicas inclinadas a salir en pos de más, o en pos de variedad, había que herrarlas de alguna manera para que permanecieran estigmatizadas—claro, por su gula orgasmática—ante todo el mundo.

Solución número dos: acuñar sustantivo denigrante y acusador. ¿De qué? Pues de mujer adicta al placer del orgasmo múltiple y variado. *¡Right on,* cachetón! LA PUTA. Con esta palabrita de cuatro letras, junto con el mito del exclusivo orgasmo, tipo pene-(preferiblemente-del-esposo)-en-el-coño, se controló el comportamiento lascivo de Evita, y Adancito quedó libre para hacerla de don Juan. Relacionado a esto prodríamos comentar el fenómeno de que no existe la forma femenina de cornudo. O sea, que la mujer que tiene más de un hombre le pone cuernos a su compañero, hecho imperdonable y de infinita vergüenza para la víctima encornada. Sin embargo, hombre que tiene mujeres extracurriculares no le pone ni cuernos ni nada a su esposa o compañera; *au contraire,* a él se le adula de ser todo un hombre; y de la esposa, en algún momento (específicamente en el velorio del esposo) se diría que fue una santa. Además, se podría comentar que relacionado a este curioso fenómeno lingüístico/cultural, existe otro, no menos curioso; a saber, no existe el equivalente masculino de ninfomaníaca. Bueno eso de sátiro ya lo había anticipado. A ver, tú dime si jamás has oído en conversación común y corriente a alguien llamar sátiro al hombre más lascivo en dado universo de discurso. Ahora dime ¿a cuántas ninfomaníacas conoces? Por lo menos 139 dices. ¡Ay chavo, con qué fineza complementas mis discursos! Ahora, para resumir: mujer dada a la promiscuidad = puta, ninfomaníaca y colocadora de cuernos. Todos signos negativos y acusadores. No obstante, a varón del mismo corte se le glorifica y se le tiene de varón ejemplar, de ídolo cultural, de héroe nacional etc. Es verdad, me he desviado un poco del tema original. Sin embargo todo tiene que ver con todo. Ahora, lo único que me queda decir referente a todo esto, es que lo que nos hace falta a las mujeres, es explorar y desarrollar el orgasmo múltiple, haciendo de él la base de una nueva ideología política. Ya me lo imaginaba. A ti te encanta la idea porque no hay nada que más te guste que facilitarme cuanto orgasmo apetezca, a como dé lugar, con o sin pene. ¿Y estás seguro que nada de complejitos por tu parte? Ay, Sergio sois una verdadera joya.

Rosalee Gurrola

Woolworth's Bra

The bra was Woolworth's finest push up black lace, with a matching panty girdle. I couldn't take my eyes off my bursting 14 1/2-year-old breasts, or the sexy pouting face my cousin had carefully designed from her Avon sampler case.

"Tonight we're going to the land of a thousand dances," Chata laughed, whirling around me while teasing my dark hair to a more sophisticated lady look. It had always been Chata's grand plan to transform me into a Party Girl, and this was the magic night. Oldies blared from her radio. "I'm your puppet," Chata sang along, then stopped, putting her hands on her waist. "I'm not gonna be any puppet. It's a new day, chica. I don't want no Mariachi wedding or ropes tied around me. I'm going to cosmetology school, then I'll get an apartment. I am The Party Girl Forever!"

I sat as if hair-sprayed to the chair, as Chata stripped, to get into her black dress. Coming from a family of three brothers and four sisters, I knew what other women looked like throughtout various stages of puberty, but had never seen such ripe beauty. Chata talked on nonchalantly, seeming unaware that I was staring at her sumptuous body. She bent slightly to pour her breasts into her bra, looked at me, then gave me a sly smile. "Blanca, have you ever had your chi chi's sucked?" Before I could answer, Chata added, "Your man will do it, and you'll love it so much, you'll let him put his pee pee in you . . . but don't get pregnant." Chata motioned to me to zip up her dress. "Do you know how to stop from having babies?"

I proudly announced, "I heard Abuela talking about cutting an orange in half and . . ."

Chata cut in laughing. "That's a screwdriver stupid! Man, I'm gonna have to teach you everything. You and your sisters are so square."

I felt my face grow warm. How Chata would laugh if she knew that I still had cut-out-girls from the Sears Catalog.

"And don't act so serious, Blanca, when we get to the party. Just laugh at everything the Home Boys say. Party up, but don't act like a *puta*."

Land of 1,000 Dances started to play on the radio. The room smelled of Aquanet and Juicy Fruit gum. I smiled at myself in the mirror, caught up in the excitement, wondering if Little Ernie would be as cute as Chata said. And would I get kissed?

Arcelia Ponce

La preferida

—Mija, cuida a Susana en lo que llevo a Leonel al doctor.
My mom had just left me with an eleven-month-old little girl to take care of. What luck! I would get to stay home from school. Now I would get to ride the bike we got from the Goodwill. I could rarely persuade my older brother and sister to let me ride it. I took Susana and set her on the handle bars of the old blue bike. At nine years of age it did not occur to me that if I fell down, the baby would also fall. There was nothing else I could do with Susana, but take her with me.

I was about to take a turn on a sharp curb when Susana and I fell to the dusty ground. She started to wail. I started rocking her up and down trying desperately to hush her up. Just then I saw my father rounding the corner into our driveway. I did not know what he was doing there. He was supposed to be at work. He had probably decided he needed to take a day off from work, like he usually did about every other week. Sometimes I wondered how my father was not fired from his job with all the days he took off.

I knew I was really going to get in trouble with my father. The only thought that ran through my head was how many *cintarazos* I was going to get this time. Maybe this time it would be more than the usual three, since I had not even cleaned the house yet and I was already playing outside. All I knew was that my father would give it to me good. After all, this was the father that as a punishment had made my brother Luis, kneel on a floor heater, and then turned it on.

—¿Qué pasa Julia?
—Me caí con Susana en la bicicleta.

My father patted my head and told me to go into the house. I could not believe he wasn't angry but I faithfully obeyed. I went into the house and rocked Susana to sleep and put her down on the tattered sofa as my father ordered me to do. My father called me to the dining room. Now, I just knew I was going to get it. He had just waited to hit me until Susana was out of the way. I felt embarrassed standing before my father. Since I knew I was not going to school that day I had not even bothered to get out of my night gown. I knew no decent girl should do that. I started to excuse myself when suddenly he came up to me, reached for my hand and pulled me towards him.

He took his big hands, that always seemed permanently stained with car grease, and cupped them over my newly developed breast. It hurt. During those days I had started to discover that changes were going on with me. I did not know why I started to get smelly at school after P.E. I did not know why my breasts hurt when I bumped against something. These were secret concerns to me. I did not like him touching my secrets. I pushed his hands away.

I should have known this was coming. It all started that ugly morning when there was no sun or rain. Everything was just a dirty gray. I had gone into my parents' bedroom and climbed into bed with them. My father pulled me to his side and covered me with the blanket. It felt good to have some attention. It was rare that I got to have my parents to myself. All of a sudden I felt his hands going into my panties. He started fondling me "down there". The pain was not the only thing that hurt. I knew daddy was not supposed to have his hands in there, but I did not know why. I did not know what to do. Every time he moved his finger I got a sick feeling in my stomach. I knew I could not tell my mom. What would she say? She would probably slap my face and say I was imagining things. Then I would be a disgrace to my family. I let my father keep on fondling. There was nothing I could do, no one I could turn to. I felt like I was drowning in an ugly, muddy lake.

But now, the man was pulling me towards his bedroom; this was not father. I knew something bad was going to happen. I tried getting away, but couldn't. He finally got me into his bedroom. Since the thin, white door did not have a lock, he took a big box and put it against the door. *Oh my God, what was going to happen? What was he going to do?* I felt more scared than I had ever before. At that moment I would rather have been in Luis's place on the heater than in that dark room with that man. The room was tiny and yet I felt I was in the middle of a world with nothing on it but dirt and a dark sky. There were no human beings except me and my father. There was no place to run to or hide. No one to turn to. I was all alone in a situation from which there was no escaping. He came up to me and took my nightgown off. Suddenly I no longer felt I was alone in the world. Now there were thousands of faces from the top of the sky staring down at my naked body. They could

Santa Barraza

Mother Looks On While Vulture Preys On Us

see everything. This man was my father. My father would not do anything to hurt me. He took my panties off. I brought my hand down to cover myself. I tried to refuse. I did not know what he was going to do, I just knew it was not right. I did not know the word *sex*, much less what it meant. I finally stopped resisting because I knew my father could not hurt me. As he opened my legs I felt a thick tar cover my heart. I knew I was no longer the same.

I could no longer go back to playing innocently with my dolls like I used to. I could no longer look at my father's face without a disgusted feeling coming over me. Everytime I looked him in the eyes I felt the fury of an animal come upon me. I felt like lashing out at him. Oh what I would have given to have had claws to tear out his eyes and tongue, which had been so big and powerful as they went through my body. That tongue which had taken me from a young budding tree to an old ugly tree, with leaves that afterwards always seemed to be in autumn. They had torn away anything clean and pure I had ever known.

In spite of my feelings I still did not understand why I hated him so much. Why was the thing he had done to me so bad? After all, he had said he was only doing it to warn me of what was going to happen when I got married. What was so wrong about him wanting to warn me? I did not know why but I hated him. I hated, hated, hated him.

My hate could not stay within the four walls of that dungeon he had thrust me into. Soon it leaked out through tiny cracks of the wall and lashed its fury upon that *man*, not my father. *Mi papá ya no me llamaba su muñeca, sino ahora me llamaba la hipócrita de la casa. Sólo porque iba a la iglesia.* My mom never defended me. *Si sólo te portaras bien, él se portaría bien contigo. Tú eres mala con él. Tú sabes que tú eres su preferida.*

Mami, ¿qué no puedes ver en mis ojos que ya no tengo la vida de una niña, sino la de una mujer que ya no quiere nada con el mundo? Mami, ¿qué no puedes ver cuando mi padre se me acerca y me tienta y yo grito que me deje en paz? No mami, no es que él esté jugando conmigo. Él está matándome poco a poco tocándome en donde no debe. Lo mismo siguió por tres malditos años. Yo no sabía lo que era.

But maybe it was for the best that I did not know. If I had known, it would have been enough to completely cut from that old peeling tree the little life that was left in it. How many times did I think of taking my life after being locked up in the bathroom, after my father broke my lips when I disagreed with him. How many times did that thought run through my head when mother denied I was her daughter.

For the next years of my life, all there was were books, books, and thirty four-hours of work at age fourteen while going to high school. Anything to forget the dirt that was inside of me. Anything to forget that day when that man opened my legs to tear away any good or love I could ever know.

Sonia Rivera-Valdés

Las historias prohibidas de Marta Veneranda
(fragmento)

Una noche, cuando tenía diecisiete años, soñé que una mujer y yo hacíamos el amor. Ella estaba desnuda y su cuerpo era muy hermoso. Aun hoy recuerdo los senos firmes y llenos y su piel que brillaba con un tono parecido al del tabaco. El sueño me inquietó mucho. En aquel entonces, mediados de 1950, estaba viendo a un sicólogo porque me deprimía frecuentemente sin saber exactamente por qué. El era un hombre soltero, de cerca de cincuenta años, que a menudo me celebraba durante las visitas a su consulta. Le conté lo que había soñado. Me preguntó si yo había pensado en "eso" alguna vez. Me imaginé que "eso" significaba ideas homosexuales y le dije que no. La forma en que hizo la pregunta, eludiendo hablar directamente, no invitaba a una exploración más profunda del tema. Me dijo que no me preocupara, aquel sueño simbolizaba otra cosa. Su opinión profesional me tranquilizó y traté de olvidar el asunto. Sin embargo, en los días que siguieron, sin poder evitarlo, cada vez que abrazaba a mi novio me preguntaba cómo se sentiría en la realidad la piel apretada y tersa de la espalda de la mujer del sueño.

En el verano de 1969 vine a vivir a Nueva York con mi marido y nuestras hijas. Había pasado mucho tiempo desde aquel sueño perturbador y lo había olvidado, o yo lo creía así. Ya las niñas estaban en edad escolar, la casa me ahogaba y necesitábamos más dinero del que mi marido ganaba. Su inglés deficiente lo incapacitaba, por el momento, para practicar su profesión. Con la recomendación de unos amigos, conseguí un empleo en una oficina pequeña en la calle Rivington, cerca de Union Square. Pagaban poco, pero casi no había que hablar inglés y aquél era un requisito imprescindible para mí. Tomé el empleo como algo temporal. Detestaba el trabajo de oficina, pero no sabía qué más hacer. De lo único que estaba segura era de que quería mucho a mis hijas y que no soportaba dedicar mi vida a los quehaceres de la casa.

Comencé a trabajar un lunes de principios de otoño. Mientras me dirigía al trabajo en aquella mañana de lluvia, pensaba que estaría cansadísima al llegar la tarde. Me había levantado a las cinco para preparar el desayuno, dejar la casa lista y llevar las niñas a la escuela. Una vecina las recogería y las cuidaría hasta que yo regresara.

Subí en el elevador del edificio donde estaba mi empleo pensando que debí haberme maquillado mejor para aquel primer día de trabajo, pero no había tenido ganas de hacerlo. El jefe, bajito y gordo, de origen irlandés, me saludó y me llevó al salón donde trabajaría. Yo sabía que la oficina tenía pocos empleados, pero no imaginé que sólo tres. A la primera que vi fue a una mujer alta y trigueña que, de pie frente a un ventanal, miraba el parque que estaba frente al edificio mientras tomaba té distraídamente. Llevaba una blusa de mangas largas y una falda de tachones planchada con esmero. Tenía el pelo negro, largo hasta el cuello y se hacía la raya a la izquierda. El jefe la llamó para presentármela.

Al volverse la mujer hacia nosotros, me llamó la atención su cara de anchos pómulos, la boca, un poco grande y de labios finos, pero sobre todo me llamaron la atención los ojos. Eran muy oscuros, más bien pequeños, rasgados y me pareció que permanecían serios aunque se sonriera como lo hacía ahora, al acercarse con la taza en la mano. Cuando meses después dejé de verla la imagen de aquella primera vez recurría fija a mi memoria. Me dijo su nombre: Zobeida; le dije el mío y los celebramos mutuamente.

Faltaban uno minutos para la hora en que se suponía que empezáramos a trabajar. Zobeida me preguntó si quería té o café. Como éramos sólo tres empleadas, la compañía los ofrecía gratis. Ella prefería té con leche. Yo jamás tomaba té, pero le dije que tomaría lo mismo. Sirvió dos tazas y nos sentamos, una al lado de la otra, en los asientos en que trabajaríamos durante las ocho horas siguientes. El té con leche se convirtió en una especie de rito que practicábamos todo el día: ella me lo preparaba a mí o yo se lo preparaba a ella.

El trabajo era el más aburrido del mundo. Lo bueno era que el jefe nunca interrumpía nuestras conversaciones si no demorábamos la tarea. Frente a nosotras se sentaba la otra empleada, una rumana como de cuarenta años alta y rubia, también recién llegada a los Estados Unidos. Era muy habladora. Me contó, inmediatamente, que en Rumania vivía en la calle principal de Bucarest en un apartamento espacioso con un gran balcón a la calle. En Nueva York vivía en un cuarto con una sola ventana que daba al interior del edificio. Todos los días se quejaba de haber venido. Se creía una beldad y pensó que al llegar al aeropuerto estaría esperándola un millonario para proponerle matrimonio, pero hasta el momento no había aparecido y empezaba a perder la paciencia. También Zobeida y yo nos impaciéntabamos con aquella historia interminable. Optamos por aparentar que estábamos ensimismadas en el trabajo hasta que se calló. Zobeida y yo comenzamos a hablar en español. Simpaticé con ella en seguida. Al llegar la tarde de aquel primer día de trabajo ya sabíamos que teníamos mucho en común. Las dos éramos cubanas, así que de lo primero que hablamos fue de la isla. Después, Zobeida era casi de mi edad, también casada desde muy joven y tenía dos niños, más o menos de la edad de las mías. A las dos nos gustaban los libros, la música, el cine. Al llegar a mi casa aquella tarde me decía que había sido amistad a primera vista. Le conté a mi marido lo simpática que era y me acosté entusiasmada con la idea de que al otro día podríamos reanudar nuestra conversación.

 Desde el primer momento Zobeida me inspiró un sentimiento raro, pero a la vez familiar, así que no pensé mucho en eso. Era familiar porque siempre, para sentirme contenta, había necesitado la amistad íntima de una mujer. Hasta cierto punto, esto era normal en mi cultura, pero en mí la necesidad era muy fuerte. Conocía mujeres para las que el marido era su mundo y las amigas un suplemento, relaciones sustituibles, agradables, pero prescindibles. Para mí nunca había sido así. Desde pequeña necesitaba compartir lo que pensaba, sentía y parte de mis actividades, con otra mujer. Uno de mis grandes placeres de siempre era sentarme a tomar café y a conversar tranquila e íntimamente con una amiga. Sin embargo, Zobeida, por alguna razón que no podía puntualizar, me intranquilizaba. Me inspiraba la simpatía y la confianza que me habían inspirado otras mujeres en el pasado, pero este sentimiento era más intenso. Era la intensidad lo que me inquietaba.

 Para Zobeida también era muy importante la amistad con mujeres. Tanto, que fue la causa de uno de los mayores problemas que había tenido con su mamá. Cuando tenía dieciocho años estaba comprometida con un muchacho. También tenía una amiga a la que estaba muy apegada y a quien conocía desde antes de ser novia del muchacho. Una vez Zobeida se enfermó, estuvo en cama por varios días y la única persona que quería ver era a la amiga. La madre se preocupó mucho por esta preferencia, al extremo de preguntar a la hija si tenía algo más que una amistad con la amiga. Zobeida le contestó que por supuesto no y pensó que la madre se había vuelto loca, pero la señora insistía en que necesitaba saber la verdad. Obligó a la hija a arrodillarse delante de ella y a jurarle que no estaba mintiendo. Zobeida recordaba aquella historia como la más humillante de su vida. Yo le pregunté por qué prefería estar con la amiga antes que con el novio. Me contestó que se sentía más acompañada con ella que con él.

En muy pocos días nos habíamos contado nuestras vidas: lugares de nacimiento de padres y abuelos, cuentos de partos, enfermedades de los niños. Las dos nos considerábamos de paso por Nueva York. No nos gustaba la ciudad para criar hijos. Queríamos un lugar más tranquilo, casas con más espacio. Su marido y el mío estaban buscando trabajo en otros estados y en Latinoamérica.

Según pasaron los días, después de contar los hechos vividos pasamos a analizarlos, porqué las cosas habían sido como fueron. Comenzamos a hablar de nuestros sentimientos y ya casi no cambiamos de tema. No éramos felices. Ambas teníamos problemas matrimoniales. Sin embargo, para los cánones de nuestra cultura, tanto su marido como el mío, eran irreprochables. No tenían amantes, no bebían, no nos pegaban, eran buenos proveedores. El problema de Zobeida, creía ella, era que sentía un vacío muy grande nacido de la indiferencia de su marido hacia el sexo en general, no sólo en sus relaciones. Su vida sexual era casi inexistente. Sin embargo, lo consideraba inteligente y sensato y tenían una buena amistad. Ya casada, había tenido un amante, pero aquello tampoco resultó; quería compartir su vida con un hombre del que estuviera enamorada. Mi problema era distinto. Mi marido y yo vivíamos, no en distintos mundos, sino en distintas galaxias. Teníamos un problema sexual en aquel momento, pero no por el sexo en sí, sino por falta de entendimiento mutuo.

Nos hicimos los cuentos de los amores pasados. Mi novio favorito había sido el primero que tuve, cuando tenía catorce años. La mejor relación de Zobeida el novio de los dieciocho años, aunque no lo quisiera ver cuando se enfermó. Decía que era un muchacho sensible y buen guitarrista. En esta parte de la historia comentábamos que era increíble que casi con treinta años cada una, no hubiéramos encontrado un hombre con quien nos sintiéramos felices: "Una mujer tan bonita como tú," decía yo. "Y como tú," decía Zobeida, y así entre lamentación y lamentación nos celebrábamos. Al terminar con los hombres del presente y del pasado, hablábamos de los del futuro. Ambas pensábamos que en algún momento nos divorciaríamos y encontraríamos al que nos haría felices. Aquí volvíamos a celebrarnos. Dos mujeres tan atractivas merecían vivir contentas.

Desde el segundo día optamos por no salir a almorzar. Traeríamos algo de la casa y comeríamos en la oficina. Teníamos poco dinero y además, la hora del almuerzo era la mejor para conversar. El jefe y la otra empleada salían, decían que necesitaban un poco de aire después de cuatro horas encerrados, pero para nosotras era más importante estar solas. A aquella hora podíamos prestar atención total a las historias de la otra. Al cabo de algunos días estábamos aisladas casi por completo de Carlota, siempre sentada frente a nosotras; tanto, que empezó a sentirse celosa porque no tenía a quien hacer sus cuentos. Cada día, sin darnos cuenta, conversábamos más bajo y acercábamos más los asientos. Por largos ratos, mientras trabajábamos, sin mirarnos, hablábamos de libros, de películas y de otras mil cosas. Pero a veces, cuando nosotras éramos el tema, al llegar a un punto más alegre o triste que el resto de la historia interrumpíamos por unos segundos la revisión de las listas y nos mirábamos fijamente a los ojos. Entonces el corazón me palpitaba más rápido y fuerte. Yo pensaba que la conversación me emocionaba demasiado, pero después pensaba que con nadie podía hablar en aquellos momentos de mis sentimientos y de mis tristezas. Era lógico que me emocionara.

Cuatro o cinco semanas después de haber comenzado a trabajar, ya estábamos en octubre, una mañana como de costumbre me paré enfrente del espejo del baño para maquillarme. Mi desgano por vestirme y pintarme había desaparecido. Me despertaba entusiasmada, pensando qué me pondría y cúal color de lápiz labial combinaría mejor con la ropa. Aquella mañana terminé con el creyón de labios y me miré despacio en el espejo para ver cómo lucía. Estaba contenta, apurada por salir. De momento, mientras me miraba a los ojos escuché una pregunta que llegó sin esperar y que sonaba ajena, como si la mujer de adentro del espejo le preguntara a la de afuera: "¿Por qué estás poniendo tanto cuidado en arreglarte?" Inmediatamente llegó otra: "¿Para quién te estás arreglando?" Y oí la contestación como viniendo de una voz que no era mía, aunque salía de adentro de mí: "Para Zobeida." Quedé paralizada. No, no era posible que yo me estuviera arreglando para otra mujer. Sin embargo, era así. De pronto, me acordé del sueño que tuve a los diecisiete años. ¿Estaría equivocado el psicólogo aquel y sí tendría que ver con deseos sexuales? ¿Sería yo homosexual? El pensamiento me angustió de una manera feroz. Sentí que una pieza se había soltado adentro de la cabeza y comenzado a girar vertiginosamente. No podía pensar claro. Mi idea del sexo entre mujeres se reducía a la historia de algún librito pornográfico que había caído en mis manos cuando era adolescente y a los cuentos que había oído de que en algunos clubes de La Habana los turistas americanos pagaban para que conocidas bailarinas de mambo tuvieran sexo delante de ellos. Nunca había oído ni leído sobre al amor entre mujeres. Las *invertidas* mencionadas de vez en cuando en las conversaciones de mi familia me parecían tan lejanas como las marcianas.

De cualquier forma, aquella mañana salí para el trabajo. Después de un rato me calmé y durante el viaje en el tren pensé que no era para tanto. Aún en el peor de los casos nadie sabía lo que pensaba y sentía. Siempre he querido ser honesta conmigo misma, así que decidí enfrentarme con mis sentimientos. Lo primero era tratar de definir qué sentía por Zobeida. De que me simpatizaba mucho, que nos llevábamos bien y me sentía muy acompañada, cuando estaba con ella no tenía duda. Pero todo eso estaba bien. Para mí la línea divisoria entre la amistad y el amor era si quería acostarme con ella. Eso, que nunca había pensado antes, era lo que tenía que averiguar. A lo mejor sí lo quería inconscientemente, me dije.

Llegué a la oficina y saludé a Zobeida, como todos los días. Después de un rato, me preguntó qué me pasaba. Le contesté que nada, que estaba bien. Pasé todo aquel día y los siguientes observándola y preguntándome si quería hacer el amor con ella. Le miraba la boca mientras hablaba o se reía y me preguntaba qué sentiría si la besaba o me besaba. La imagen del beso me resultaba inconcebible. No podía imaginarme besándola. Después de interrogarme de manera obsesiva, siempre con la misma respuesta, me convencí a mí misma de que no quería aquello. Al cabo de interminables meditaciones Romaind Rolland, el escritor francés, vino al rescate. Recordé que había dicho que la amistad es un enamoramiento de las almas. Eso era lo que yo sentía por Zobeida y no tenía que sentirme culpable. De allí en adelante, cada día estuvimos más unidas. Por la tarde, siempre íbamos juntas hasta el tren y en la puerta nos separábamos porque tomábamos distinto rumbo. Pero un día se nos ocurrió que podíamos irnos de tiendas por quince o veinte minutos, no más, porque siempre estábamos apuradas por llegar a la casa. Le dije a la vecina que me cuidaba las niñas que los trenes estaban imposibles, que le pagaría el tiempo extra cada vez que me demorara. A mi marido, que siempre llegaba después que yo, le hice el mismo cuento. Zobeida habló con su mamá, que le cuidaba los niños y le dijo algo parecido. Casi nunca comprábamos. Íbamos de departamento en departamento mirando, consultándonos gustos y precios y conversando. Poco a poco se fue haciendo más difícil separarnos. En vez de veinte minutos comenzamos a quedarnos media hora.

Una mañana llegué y Zobeida, que generalmente llegaba antes que yo, tomaba té junto al ventanal como el día que la conocí. Era viernes y no nos veríamos durante el fin de semana. Me acerqué y le dije que en el camino se me había ocurrido algo. Ella, sin titubear, me dijo: "Que hoy cuando salgamos por la tarde nos vayamos a sentar en el parque un rato." La miré estupefacta. Nunca nos habíamos sentado en el parque. No podía creer que ella lo había dicho, antes de que yo lo dijera, exactamente lo que pensaba. Le respondí: "¿Cómo tú lo sabías?" Respondió mirándome a los ojos: "¿Sabes que me estoy asustando?"

De aquel día en adelante, cambiamos las tiendas por el parque. Total, nunca comprábamos, en el parque conversaríamos más cómodas. Hablábamos de los temas de siempre y de los pequeños sucesos de la vida diaria, pero las conversaciones fueron haciéndose difíciles, con silencios frecuentes en que nos mirábamos a los ojos por unos segundos y cambiábamos la vista a los árboles que se estaban quedando desnudos, o hacíamos algún comentario sobre el bonito color de las hojas que cubrían el césped y las aceras. Poco a poco dejamos de hablar de los maridos, de los hombres en general, de libros, de películas, de la casa y hasta de los hijos. A veces permanecíamos sentadas, una al lado de otra, por espacio de varios minutos sin decir nada. Yo quería estar con ella, estar con ella, estar con ella. Nada más me importaba, pero estar con ella ¿para qué? No se me ocurría nada. A menudo me entraban ganas de llorar. Lo mismo le sucedía a ella; entonces pensábamos que era la situación de nuestros matrimonios que iban de mal en peor. Había que encontrar una solución. Teníamos que buscar un hombre de quien enamorarnos, concluimos. En vez de buscar hombres comenzamos a visitarnos los domingos. A veces yo iba a su casa con niñas y marido y a veces ella venía a la mía con su séquito familiar. Ya era noviembre. A pesar de que comenzaba a enfriar demasiado para sentarse en el parque y casi nadie lo hacía, nosotras seguimos haciéndolo. Hasta los vagabundos y drogadictos escaseaban, pero nosotras acudíamos cada tarde y siempre nos demorábamos unos minutos más antes de separarnos. Llegué a pensar que no quería ni a mis hijas porque ellas me obligaban a llegar temprano a la casa. Sin embargo, continuaba trabajando, haciendo los quehaceres de la casa y dándole un beso a mi marido cuando llegaba por la noche.

Para fines de aquel mes, al marido de Zobeida le notificaron que lo habían aceptado para un trabajo que había solicitado en el norte de la Florida. Comenzaría a principios de diciembre. Se irían después de Thanksgiving. Me dijo que como no sabíamos a dónde iríamos a parar en el futuro, con destinos tan inseguros como los nuestros, debíamos pensar en una manera de garantizar que si perdíamos contacto y queríamos recuperarlo, podríamos hacerlo. Siempre yo podía llamar a una tía suya establecida en Nueva York desde hacía muchos años y que no se mudaría. Ella me diría donde estaba Zobeida.

El último viernes que fue a trabajar, cuando salimos, la acompañé en el tren hasta la estación donde se bajaba. Estábamos paradas una frente a la otra, sin hablar. Cuando se iba a bajar, sin haber dicho nada antes, dijo: "Yo lo he pensado mucho y creo que lo mejor es que me vaya porque si no, esto se va a complicar." No nos besamos ni siquiera como se besan las amigas cubanas, que frotan una cara contra la otra sin intervención de la boca. Me apretó un hombro con la mano para despedirse y nos miramos muy fijo hasta que se abrieron las puertas del tren. Sentí, en aquel momento sí lo sentí, que no quería que se fuera así, sin abrazarnos, sin que ni siquiera nuestras manos hubieran podido palpar una vez la piel de la otra. Sentí que el corazón me latía en la garganta y que iba a llorar con grandes sollozos, pero no lo hice. Continué en el tren camino a mi casa, repitiéndome sin hablar aquellas últimas palabras y sintiendo en mi hombro el apretón de despedida.

Algún tiempo después yo también me mudé de Nueva York. Zobeida y yo nos escribimos unas cuantas veces preguntándonos por la familia y contando los progresos en la escuela de los niños de cada una. Después perdimos contacto. Pasaron aun varios años antes de que me divorciara y entendiera que quería compartir mi vida con una mujer. Al hacerlo me sentí mejor madre y mejor persona, más integrada conmigo misma.

Nunca he vuelto a tomar té con leche, ni he visto más a Zobeida. Pero un día me gustaría buscarla y sentarme a conversar con ella. Tengo entendido que se divorció, se casó con otro y después se volvió a casar con el primer marido. No sé como piensa hoy en día ni si recuerda las tardes en el parque. Me gustaría preguntárselo.

Victoria Alegría Rosales

To All Women Who Have Followed the Same Road As I

There are many things that irritate me in life now that I'm forty-eight, an age when I should be mellow and at peace with myself. Two of the things that irritate me are to hear about sexual abuse and to be told that I don't look like a Mexican.

Though I grew up in Mexico, and went to school with other Mexicans and have many Mexican friends, I still do not know what a Mexican is supposed to look like. Someone remarked to me once that I don't look like the Mexican women picking grapes.

I know how the Mexican women who worked in the fields looked. They were much browner than myself because of the many hours in the sun. They had husbands and they had many children. I knew how my kind, who worked in the fields looked, when they came home. They were tired from working but had to cook dinner, tend the children, do the groceries with the husband, the laundry by themselves. Some of the men were good fathers. Others were alcoholics, drug or child abusers, wife beaters. I was one of those abused housewives.

My ex-husband, Harry, was a wife beater. Harry was an American, born in San Diego, California. It took me five years to make up my mind to leave him. I didn't know who was going to pay the rent and take care of the children. I had no job, no skills. I could hardly speak English. I didn't know there were social workers that could have helped. I was nineteen and he was twenty-two when we got married.

Harry would lie down on top of me, spitting on my face as he asked, "Do you love me?" If I said, no, he would continue spitting. If I said yes, he would stick his hard swollen penis into me, yelling in my ear, "puta," or "whore." If I cried, he would slap me. If I held my tears, he'd put the weight of his one hundred seventy-five pounds upon me until I passed out. How did I survive? I don't know. Was this love? I asked myself many times. If not, what was it?

I used to look at myself in the mirror, but I couldn't see who I was. I could only see a shadow of my skinny beat-up body with bruises, tears, mucus streaming, lips trembling. Harry would say, "You are ugly. Stupid. I don't know why I married a dumb Mexican."

One day when Harry beat me up I asked why he married me. He replied that because he thought my parents had money and because I was a good fuck. "By marrying you I lost my chance of becoming a concert pianist," he said, showing me a yellow clipping of him as an eleven-year-old boy shaking hands with Arthur Rubenstein. What was I to do? I must not have any more children. Two were more than enough. Harvey was born in 1959 and Alton, a new year's baby in 1963. How was I going to prevent pregnancy if I was forced into bed. I didn't know about contraceptives, moon cycles, birth control pills. "Come to fuck," Harry would order.

Deep inside of me, I knew I musn't let my spirit die. But how was I going to get away from Harry? I didn't know. I wanted to learn something, be different from the Mexican housewives. I wanted to have a goal instead of an abusive husband and a child every year. I wanted to go to school instead of church. I wanted to be myself, find someone, raise my children, live in peace.

I began learning English by listening to the TV Harry brought home to watch sports. Later I learned how to drive Harry's '53 Buick with an automatic transmission. Learning was easy. The first time, I drove three blocks. As I became more confident, I went further. One night I entered the freeway. Each moment I had, I studied for the written driver's test. It took me several times before I got my license.

When Paul, Harry's father offered babysitting, I enrolled in a nearby high school. A teacher became interested in my pronunciation. I was learning English. Some day I might get a job, support my children, pay my own bills.

I was happy when my school assignments improved. I was beginning to find out about how to become free. I had a friendly teacher.

The Mexican housewives, working in the fields seemed so different.

Mary I. Siqueiros

First Time

I cannot remember if it was morning or afternoon, but would say that it was around noontime. I was living in an old house that had an upstairs. The bathroom was in the back house, off of a washroom. I can remember back stairs. I must've been in the back yard and felt something that made me go to the bathroom. Whether it was sticky or what is not clear. I know I spoke to my mother. Did we have sanitary napkins at home? Don't know, but I presume we did because my mother was still young enough to use them. I know we used pins, until we could get to a store so she could buy me a "sanitary belt". (A mystery at the time she mentioned it to me.)

Then I learned how to wrap a piece of newspaper around "it" and how to tuck the end of the newspaper in, so it would not unwrap itself.

I cannot remember if the *Kotex* were kept in the bathroom or not. I can remember how it would smell, and the blood would dry around the sides of the *Kotex* when you could not afford to change *too* often, because you were going to run out of *Kotex*. Oh, the very first time my mother made me a pad out of rags, because we didn't have any *Kotex*.

In later years I can remember my stepfather making comments like, "I am going broke because of having to buy those things!" (In total, there are seven females in the family.)

Another problem was sending someone to the store to buy *Kotex*. When my brother was little there was no problem, but after he got older, he refused to go. Naturally, I did not want to go because I did not have anything to put on.

I disliked "rags" because they were heavy and cumbersome. You could never get them folded right. If you used *too* thin a rag then blood would seep through right away AND if you folded it thick, it felt horrible to walk! You walked with your legs spread apart and you had to walk with a "straddle!"

I also remember my stomach feeling queasy and maybe gurgling a little bit. With queer little backaches. I remember hating to wash the dried blood off of my pubic hair. *(Why was I doing that? Had I not changed often or what?)* I do not remember my mother filling me in on the story of menstruation at all, and here I get a little confused as to what was said and not said.

Mainly I thought of it as a nuisance, always coming when I had more important things to do. Always a traumatic thing. . . . *Who was going to go to the store and buy them?* I do not remember telling my sisters. (I am the oldest sister.) I do not recall saying, "Hey! Do you know I am menstruating?" I do not think I would've used the term "menstruating". I do not remember using the term, "my monthly". I think I used to say "sick". I just seem to remember my brother's curiosity whenever anyone was "sick" and HE had to run to the store!!!

Rita Chávez — Who Can We Be?

Mary I. Siqueiros

My Other Self
(Journal entry, Fall 1970)

Have you ever had something so wrong with you as to be right? That's the way I feel. Guess I have been leading up to this since a little girl, when to play Daddy was the big thing with me. Finding women's things to do is just not in the cards for me. The bad thing is not being accepted by the people on the edge of the world. The twilight sense of this is what's wrong. Why can't you be able to live without love and affection? Then life could get going without complications or being tempted by words, actions or deeds.

Life has to be made up of terror, cause that's all I feel in thinking of continuing it. To have to leave thoughts of children and a homelife that's acceptable in some kind of limbo, because that's what will have to be done. Life, for me will have to become a routine thing, one for the day, and one for the night. Of course, right now I know that after tonight more definite decisions will have to be made. They must've been started quite a while ago, must've been when I decided to come to the "Gay" town. Knowing that I was leaving so other people wouldn't get hurt. Mothers are the worst of all. The hard thing to say is, "My child is different." Because different is what I am.

Maybe I am assuming too much. Maybe other people do have these feelings but can control or hide them better. Maybe all those people in the "crazy" house have the right idea. There you can be relieved of all the right and wrong sense of your feelings and just "feel." Without any pretense because you are not quite right.

To be right. A routine, standard, wholesome girl, would be my wish. But, wishes are not to be granted just for the asking, so to make this life livable, my idea or rule will be one of tragedy. Sent to roam the world in some kind of atonement. For who, I don't know. Maybe for the world in general.

Carmen Tafolla

Federico y Elfiria

Pos, he liked her jus cause of that. No le hacía que era muy ranchera y nunca había visto más que su casa. She was a good girl, which is like saying that she wasn't a bad girl, or not even a little bad, y'know?

The first time Federico started liking Elfiria was the day Chato and Manuel were teasing him and said that Federico se vestía muy galán, that a lo mejor he was trying to impress the girls... and then Manuel said that a lo mejor there was somebody he was already talking to a las escondiditas and Chato (to impress Manuel) said he'd seen Elfiria writing notes with big hearts that said *Federico plus Elfiria.* And they both laughed a lot at Federico and Federico got red. He knew that a lo mejor Chato was just making it up but de todos modos he wondered. I mean, it was real embarrassing. I mean, Elfiria was the kind of girl that didn't *like* nobody. She just went home from school and did what her parents said. And she wasn't the kind of girl that anyone went around *liking* either. I mean she was just somebody who sat in that desk and whose name got called too before his on the roll, and that's the only way anyone thought of her, y'know? But just the same he wondered.

And I mean she'd never had any boyfriends or anything and you knew she was a good girl (which is to say, not a bad girl).

Well, the next day Manuel and Chato were talking about the baseball game with Concho Mines High and how were they gonna lose now that Pato had joined the Air Force, and they had forgotten all about the love notes and the teasing. Federico remembered, but he wasn't gonna say anything. And then he started noticing how Elfiria always had her hair so neatly braided in a trenza and none of the hairs ever loose and it always fell right down the middle of her back between the rounded shoulders. Well, he didn't know for certain if they were rounded but he'd read something like that once and they looked kind of round (como estaba ella media llenita), but that was O.K. because everybody always made fun of guys that went with girls that were flacas and called them *Bone Chompers,* and things like that. And I mean, nobody was gonna call her *La Gorda* of the class 'cause that was María de los Socorros and there were lots of others almost as fat. Besides, good girls were supposed to be a little llenitas so they wouldn't look like those mujeres in the movies who were definitely *not* good girls.

Still, he wondered. And once when he was home alone and no one was looking, he drew a little heart (in the corner of an old homework paper that he was going to throw away) and wrote *Federico + Elfiria* on it. And looked at it, just to see what it looked like (if she had done it, which she probably hadn't 'cause she was a good girl) and he liked the way Elfiria had an *F* and an *R* in it, just like Federico. And he noticed how she made her *F*'s kind a nice and open, even when they were *F*'s on somebody's paper. An then, one day, Elfiria started looking at him. (Yea, he looked at her lots, but he only did it when he was sure she didn't see, so it couldn't be that.)

■   ■   ■

About a year after they were married, he saw this movie. Not dirty, dirty, tú sabes, but it had lots a good parts in it. He came home all excited. Elfiria estaba lavando el piso and he could see her nalgas pointing at him y también esas cosas hanging down. Pos, que se reventó el globo, and he was all over her. And him going for her and her fighting him off, kinda (in her feelings), but not saying *no*, ('cause she was a good girl and s'posed to let her husband do things like that) and he was real excited, 'cause he knew that's what good girls were s'posed to do (but not do) if they were married. And he started kissing her lots, just kinda forgetting himself. And she even quit making faces for awhile. And he was real excited and breathing on her neck hard, like when he—well, you know, did it—an' pos, they did, an' just when he was about to—well, you know, venir—he just grabbed her neck and kissed it with his teeth and tongue sucking hard. I don't know why, maybe it was just seeing it in the movie that made him do it, but he didn't do it on purpose. An then he—pos estaba viniendo—and she could feel it, you could tell, and she did something that really surprised Federico—she grabbed his head in both her hands and kissed him real hard on the lips.

Well, they were both real sleepy after that and didn't think too much about it that night, but the next day, Federico was still turning this over in his head. I mean she'd never acted like that before. (He hadn't either, but then he'd seen this love movie, so that was why.) And then he started wondering if maybe she'd seen a movie too or something. I mean, she was supposed to be home during the day and he hadn't heard nothing about her going out to movies. And this started to get his little hairs on his neck up and prickly until he realized she didn't have no way to get to no movie. And then he relaxed.

But then Elfiria got up and started to get dressed and when she took her robe off, the most horrible thing happened. Right in front of him there was this dark, dark blue mark on her neck and he *knew* what it looked like.

He'd seen those before (at school) but only on bad girls. It looked every bit like a hicky.

And I guess it was O.K., what with his being her husband and all, but still—it looked funny and it bothered him. Manuel had always said, "Any girl that lets a guy give her a hicky is una *desas*." That night, Federico was still feeling bothered by it and for some reason didn't feel like going home right away. I mean he wasn't angry at her or anything, he said, he just wanted to stay out late. After all, he was a man, he could do that if he wanted. It was her business, cosa de viejas, staying home, and he went over to the cantina. He didn't go in, 'cause he didn't have but 40 cents on him and that was for Coke to go with his taquitos tomorrow lunch, but still he went to the cantina, and he parked outside in the troquita his brother gave him, and he just watched from the dark. And when it was real late, he went home.

But she was still awake and that pissed him off. And worse, she was looking at him, nice-like, and like she wanted to do something. He just went around the bed, the other side, se quitó los zapatos, and took his shirt and pants off quick, leaving his camiseta and underwear on, and slipped under the covers, facing the other way and looking asleep. She was in her gown and she curled up right against him, (¡Ingrata! ¡So he could feel her!), and his heart was going double, but he didn't move a muscle, except for squeezing his eyes more shut, to look more asleep.

Pos, if esa ingrata doesn't squeeze up against him even more, like hinting. And she stays like that, several seconds (or maybe hours), and he's so he can't take it anymore and finally—all angry he hits her with "¡Cabrona! ¡Que I'm asleep!" And she's so scared 'cause he's never called her anything like that before, that she doesn't know whether to move away or how, and so she stays absolutely still. And he's so mad that he had to speak that he keeps his eyes even more shut and his body even more still (so she can't say he's awake). And they stay that way the whole night—scrunched up against each other, his eyes squeezed shut, hers scared open, both of them scared to move an inch, and him with a hard-on and her hungry.

Bueno, that kind of did it. I mean, a man can only take so much, you know? I mean, a wife is s'posed to respect him, do what he wants when he wants, and not go bothering him otherwise, y'know?

And for the rest of that week, Federico went to the cantina every evening after work and stayed outside, parked in his troquita, and came home late and slept in his underwear, and Elfiria went to bed quietly, with her eyes open all night long.

Well, by the end of the week, they both looked pretty bad, but Federico looked the worst. Missing supper and not getting much sleep was really draining him. And Elfiria was looking O.K., but pretty sad, and never said much—even more so than usual, and she usually didn't say much.

So one day, Federico thought, "Forget the cantina, I'm going home for supper." And Elfiria was so surprised, she ran around fixing supper as quick as she could, and they both are, and without a word, he just went to the bedroom, pulled his clothes off (even his underwear—¡ya le calaba!) and went to sleep. She did too. And they slept kinda comfortable. I don't know why, but maybe they were just too tired to care about the rest.

The next day was Saturday and things felt O.K. I mean, really quiet, but they did the work they needed to do, and then come evening they ate and Federico went to bed early again. He sat and thought for awhile, and wondered about that hicky of Elfiria's but when she finished the dishes and came to lie down too, he noticed that it had faded almost away, and that made him feel better, so he drifted off to sleep.

Elfiria was really worried about Federico. I mean, she wanted to be a good wife and she sure didn't like this business of him being angry, so she resolved to try not to do anything to upset him anymore. Still, she thought about that one night lots, and how she had felt hot and shivery all over, and she tried not to think about it too much, but she fell asleep thinking about it anyway.

It was maybe 2 A.M. and they'd slept for several hours already when suddenly Elfiria found herself dreaming half-awake and hungry and felt him hard and, just tired of waiting, she pushed herself up against him and helped it along. And when Federico woke up, her hand was pushing his mouth against her neck and her—well, all the different parts of her were rubbing against him, and it all felt real good, for about about 20 minutes, until he came. And then, he started realizing—well, he wasn't too certain what, but realizing it anyway.

An he looked real quick to see if she had a hicky. And she didn't (or not that he could see in this light anyway) and that made him feel a little better.

But *still* . . .

And he fell asleep, but the next day he was worse upset than ever, and made her go to *misa*, while he stayed home and thought. Pos then if she doesn't up and hit him that week—right in the middle of his confusion—con que she's pregnant. At first, Federico was even more confused—and irritated que la ingrata had gone and gotten herself that way right now, when he was trying to figure something else out. But then, when everybody found out, and all the guys patted him on the back and said que ya era tiempo and Polos said his wife was expecting their second, and they all congratulated him, Federico felt pretty good. But still, Federico wondered. And the next day, stayed away from work so he could watch the house from behind the bushes, to see if somebody else was coming to visit her.

The sun got pretty hot, y ya le andaban las moscas y el polvo, but he was determined to find out once and for all whether she was a good girl. Pos if he didn't end up staying there hasta las 2 de la tarde, y lo único que vió was that Elfiria hung all his clothes on the line first, and then the toallas, and then her clothes. And then she gave the sobras al gato vecino. But most of the time it was just him and the moscas, sufriendo del calor. At 2, he decided that she wasn't gonna do anything anymore porque a esa hora she listened to her novela and if she was gonna do anything, she wouldn't have made it at that time, 'cause she'd miss *Amor de Lejos*. So he decided it was his baby, and, relieved, he left, sin decirle nada.

He began to feel real good about her being pregnant, and as she got bigger each month, it made him feel more like uno de los hombres que eran middle-aged y bien respected. Y ella se portó bien también, nomás que around her fifth month she started getting real wet and hungry at night, y ¡híjole! pregnant y todo, qué desgracia, pero what could he do? I mean a man can only hold back so much, and there she was, *pushing* him to do it! He didn't like the idea and he didn't *agree* with it at all—pero he was just too tired and turned on to fight it all the time. So he'd go ahead and do it, and just agree with himself in the morning that it shouldn't be that way, you know, and that it wasn't his fault.

When the time came for him to take her to the hospital, she was screaming and all that woman kind of stuff. Federico tried to be strong for her, but then as they were walking in the door, her water broke, y se mió allí, a chorros. "Elfa, can't you wait!" le regañó in a whisper, embarrassed that the nurses should see his wife letting it all go like that. I guess Elfiria didn't hear him, cause she kept right on doing it, and her dress and the floor were all wet. And then he realized it had nothing to do with her going to the bathroom, and the nurse called for a wheelchair, and Federico's stomach felt funny (probably from the leftovers at supper last night) and he slumped onto the check-in counter with a color on his face Elfiria had never seen. For a second, Elfiria forgot her pains and just stared at him in shock, then she caught him just before he went to the floor, and pushed him into the wheelchair, saying to the nurse, "Cuídamelo."

When he came to, she had already been taken in, behind those doors and the nurse just smiled and said, "We'll let you know when you can go in."

Sometime around midnight, the doctor came in to both of them, a yawning old man with a look como si hubiera comido algo that didn't taste good, saw her still in labor and said, half to the nurse and them and half to the clipboard, "Let's quit all this nonsense and get that baby out. I've got a golf game early tomorrow. She's been in labor 5 hours already—prep for C-section." Federico was about to feel fear coming on when he was interrupted by this loud voice, strangely familiar, yet totally alien. "¡NO SEÑOR!" It was Elfiria! Talking to the doctor like that! "If you can't help me, then go home and let my mother come!"

It was a boy. Named after him. Federico was in shock. He'd thought about her being pregnant, but he'd never really thought about the baby! Su hijo. Claro que era su hijo—he was named Federico, Jr., wasn't he? And when he looked at him for the first time, and saw this little person, all alive y pataleando, he just said, "I did that!?" and melted into a little pool of pride and tenderness.

Manuel had come pa' estar con él, "How ya doin', man?

Compa'! *Papá!*—and saw Federico's eyes water up as he answered, "God, I feel . . . good." Manuel, smug over the birth of his own daughter two months earlier, smiled, muy compañero, and teased, "You feel good huh? Oh, and it gets *better*, hombre. Míja 'ta más chula . . .' And you feel good now? Just wait till Elfiria gets all healed up and starts *wanting* you again—¡Uy!" he laughed and nudged Federico. Federico laughed, but it was only from the face out, porque what Manuel had said had really bothered him. Y ni le dieron the time to absorb that when Elfiria was back in her room and ready for company . . .

Fred Jr. kept them both so busy that Federico didn't have much time to think about his earlier problems with Elfiria, until one day, about 7 weeks later, when she comes up to him, real suavecito-like, y'know, and says, "Hace mucho tiempo. I'm healed now, tú sabes, down there . . ." Federico was touched, but, muy caballero, comforts, "That's O.K. honey. I don't need it. I can wait some more." The dam burst, and Elfiria, tired and glad the baby was finally asleep, burst too. "But *I* need it! *I* can't wait some more!" Federico was stunned. ". . . But . . . you . . . hombre! I always thought you were . . ." he gulped and said it directo, ". . . a good girl."

"¡Ya para con estas tonterías! Of course I'm a good girl! I'm more than that! Soy una madre—the mother of our *child* y soy tu esposa—wife, you know. Like married?"

Federico had never thought of it that way. He had always heard of pos, tú sabes—*desas*, bad girls, y también of course de good girls—but of someone being a good girl plus more? Maybe that explained it. Maybe eso de ser mother and wife let her do these kinds of things *plus* be a good girl. He hadn't figured it out completely, pero Elfiria interrupted him and said, "¡Ya olvídate de esas cosas! Let's go to bed!" And they did, and pos, tú sabes, a man can only do so much all by himself.

Xochiquetzal

Juana Alicia

Ana María Simo

What Do You See?

What Do You See? premiered at Theater for the New City, New York, on May 23, 1986, directed by the author, with Sheila Dabney as Sarah and Marek Johnson as Emily. The music was composed and performed by Beat Music. The play was one of *The Box Plays* by members of INTAR's Hispanic Playwrights-in-Residence Laboratory, Maria Irene Fornes, Director. It was done later that year at INTAR Theatre and at the Public Theatre's Festival Latino.

A run-down tenement on Forsythe Street, New York City, 1986.
SARAH: *a Black woman, late 20's; works as a cook in neighborhood restaurant.*
EMILY: *a white woman, late 20's; currently unemployed.*

Scene One

SARAH *and* EMILY's *single-room tenement apartment, Summer, 1986. Night is falling.* EMILY *has just finished making some clay figures and is putting them on the window sill.* SARAH *watches her.*

SARAH: *(Sings)*
  Yesterday I noticed
  That you have small ears and big hands
  You sat by the window
  Looking ugly in your white shirt
  Then very beautiful
  Then very beautiful
  Then very beautiful.
  You have the dirtiest fingernails
  In the Lower East Side
  The hardest face to remember
  The hardest to forget.
  I was nailed to the floor
  I was struck in the mouth

I was kicked out of breath
I was left without words
I was left without soul
When I opened my door for you.

Blackout

Scene Two

Same place, Fall 1986. EMILY *is beating egg whites with a fork to make meringue.* SARAH *reads a Kung-Fu magazine.*

SARAH: You can't do that.
EMILY: Why not? Is there a law against it?
SARAH: Yes. Mine. You're wasting a dozen eggs on that shit. Do you realize those eggs are all we have to eat?
EMILY: We'll eat the meringue.
SARAH: You're gonna end up in a shelter.
EMILY: Just because I like sweets? (SARAH *grabs the fork from* EMILY's *hand.*) Give me that fork.
SARAH: No.
EMILY: Come on. I know you want to give it back to me. You just don't know how.
SARAH: I'll give it back if you fix me an omelette.
EMILY: Too late. I put sugar in it.
SARAH: That doesn't matter. All you have to do now is add the yolks, salt, pepper and a little garlic.
EMILY: Garlic and sugar in an omelette?
SARAH: I'm a cook, remember? I get paid money to cook not one but a hundred, two hundred omelettes everyday.
EMILY: With garlic and sugar? Are you crazy?
SARAH: Ever heard of sweet and sour? Chinese, Japanese, Korean, Indian... The whole world eats sweet and sour.
EMILY: Maybe. But I can't stand it when you eat garlic. You stink for a week and not only in your mouth.
SARAH: Wanna see what I do with your fucking fork?
EMILY: I don't care.
SARAH: Good! Because I'm gonna dump it out the window.
EMILY: Give that fork, you fucking asshole!
SARAH: *(Leaning out the window with a fork).* Hey you!

EMILY: *(Trying to wrestle the fork out of* SARAH's *hand).* I'll kill you if you lose it.
SARAH: *(Shouting out the window).* Hey, you! Want a nice fork? You can eat with it or stick it up your ass! Who cares!
EMILY: Fucking cunt... This is it. I'm going to destroy you!
SARAH: Yo, man! Real silver coming down—only touched rich bitch's mouth! She got no diseases! She's clean! I know because I fuck her!
EMILY: Shut up! *(A woman's body flies by the window on its way down to the pavement, where it crashes).*
SARAH: What was that?
EMILY: A dog.
SARAH: No. It's a woman. (SARAH *looks out the window, into the pavement below).* A woman. (EMILY *tries to look.* SARAH *stops her).* Don't look, baby. There's blood everywhere.
EMILY: I want to see her.
SARAH: She's smashed on the sidewalk.
EMILY: Let me see her, please. I have to see her. (EMILY *pushes* SARAH *away and gets to the window.* SARAH *sits on the floor, crying).* Her head's cracked open like an egg and there're pieces of her brain all over the sidewalk. Her legs are broken. Her hair's spread around her face. Her eyes are open. *(To* SARAH) Why are you crying?
SARAH: I wonder who's gonna be next. (EMILY *embraces* SARAH).
EMILY: *(Sings).*
　In my neighborhood
　It's not birds or bees that fly by the window
　But women
　Wailing on their way down to the pavement
　Like dogs hit by a truck.
　Cotton dresses fly by the window in the Spring
　When cleaning house makes lives even emptier.
　Cheap coats fly in Winter
　When six months of dampness and darkness sets in the hearts.
　The fire escapes are crumbling.
　Children have year-long colds.
　Only the pushers have rosy cheeks.
　A long red ponytail and a pale face fly down
　They wash her blood from the sidewalk with flat beer
　and piss.
　Wail, wham, slam, splatter.

Another bitch bites the dust.

Blackout

Scene Three

Same place, Winter 1986. EMILY *is putting her dirty clothes in a laundry bag.* SARAH *opens the front door and watches her for a moment from the threshold.*

EMILY: What do you want?
SARAH: I just want to talk to you for a moment.
EMILY: Close the door.
SARAH: Do you mind if I sit down?
EMILY: Why do you talk to me like that? As if we didn't know each other?
SARAH: I'm trying to be nice to you. I'm trying not to start a fight.
EMILY: What do you want?
SARAH: I have something to tell you.
EMILY: What?
SARAH: I'm moving out tomorrow morning.
EMILY: Why?
SARAH: You know why: because we can't live together.
EMILY: If you leave, I'm not letting you come back. If you leave I don't want you back.
SARAH: I won't come back.
EMILY: You won't come back?
SARAH: No. I found an apartment. I paid the deposit. I signed the lease.
EMILY: Why?
SARAH: You just said that you didn't want me.
EMILY: Why?
SARAH: I don't want to talk about that again.
EMILY: But I want to.
SARAH: We've had the same conversation a hundred times.
EMILY: Then let's not have the whole conversation, let's just go to the end, where I say: "You could stay here, we could work things out here."
SARAH: Nothing will ever get worked out if we're both stuck in here.

EMILY: You used to like my hands.
SARAH: You have lovely hands.
EMILY: Lovely? What has lovely got to do with it? You liked them because they could lift you off and throw you in bed.
SARAH: You never did that to me.
EMILY: No. But I thought a lot about it. I also thought I'd pretend to drown in the bathtub, to scare you. But I never did that either.
SARAH: You can scare me if you want to. We're still lovers.
EMILY: Is that what we are?
SARAH: Yes.
EMILY: Why? How? We're not even going to live together anymore, we never make love, we never touch each other anymore, we don't even kiss...
SARAH: Why do you say that?
EMILY: Because it's the truth!
SARAH: We never stopped making love. It just didn't happen as often as it used to. Maybe now that I'm moving out we'll start doing it as before.
EMILY: I doubt it. *(Pause)*. What did you do with my earrings?
SARAH: *(Taking the earrings out of her pocket)*. I have them here.
EMILY: Why aren't you wearing them?
SARAH: I don't know.
EMILY: Don't you like them anymore?
SARAH: *(Trying to put the earrings on)*. I like them.
EMILY: *(Taking the earrings from SARAH's hands and putting them on her)*. Let me do it. You never do it right. You always tighten them up too much and your ears get red. Then you can't wear them for weeks. *(Pause)*. You need a haircut.
SARAH: Could you do it?
EMILY: Is that what a lover means to you? Someone who puts on earrings and gives haircuts?
SARAH: Yes, among other things.
EMILY: Like what?
SARAH: Breakfast! I hate to make breakfast for myself!
EMILY: Then eat out. Get a roommate. You don't need me for that.
SARAH: I hate sleeping by myself.
EMILY: You chose to.
SARAH: Yes.
EMILY: Then don't complain.
SARAH: I want to come back.

EMILY: But you just found an apartment!
SARAH: After I leave tomorrow, I want to come back three times a week: Monday, Thursday and Saturday night.
EMILY: So we can do the laundry together?
SARAH: I love you.
EMILY: You love me?
SARAH: Yes.
EMILY: You love me? Then show it to me. Don't talk so much about it. Do something. Touch me. Let me touch you. Let me touch you. Let me touch you.
SARAH: I can't do anything when you get like this.
EMILY: That's how I am. That's me!
SARAH: But I love you.
EMILY: Not me. It's not me that you love. You can't stand me. I scream. You don't like that. And I want to fuck when I feel like. You don't like that either.
SARAH: Shut up! Don't you want me back?
EMILY: No.
SARAH: You don't?
EMILY: No, I don't. Yes, I do. But not three times a week. I don't want to be your roommate. I don't even want to be your friend.
SARAH: What do you want?
EMILY: I want it as it was at the beginning.
SARAH: Okay. Let's try. Please...
EMILY: No.
SARAH: Why not?
EMILY: It won't be the same. It'll be very sad, like seeing a bad movie after reading the book: it'll destroy the book.
SARAH: What if the movie is not so bad after all?
EMILY: It usually is.
SARAH: I love you.
EMILY: Don't tell me any more. I don't want to hear it. Please.
SARAH: I have to tell you because it's the truth: I love you.
EMILY: I know. I love you too.

(They look at each other for a moment, then at the dirty clothes scattered on the floor).

SARAH: What are we going to do?
EMILY: I don't know.

SARAH: *(Starting to put dirty clothes in the laundry bag).* Can I help you?
EMILY: You don't understand, Sarah.
SARAH: I do. I do understand. *(She stands up, puts the bag on her shoulder and exits. She reenters immediately, throwing the bag in the middle of the room).*
SARAH: *(Sings)*
I wanna take my clothes to the laundromat tonight
But I can't.
The door is blocked by an army of pushers
The scum, slime, filth, shit, dirt—20 of them—
All Hispanic males
I hate them.
I'd machine gun them out of this world, gladly.
There's no bad word bad enough to call them by.
Words are too human.
Jail's home sweet home for them: they love it.
Slow torture of the soul is what they should get.
Slow soul washing, slow soul washing, slow soul washing
Until remorse spreads in their hearts like an army of crabs
Until remorse eats their flesh and cleans their souls.
Slow soul washing, slow soul washing, slow soul washing.
The law knows nothing about remorse
The law don't to the laundromats in the middle of the night.
Slow soul washing, slow soul washing, slow soul washing.
EMILY: You don't understand, Sarah.
SARAH: I do! I do understand!

Blackout

Peggy Job

La sexualidad en la narrativa femenina mexicana 1970-1987: Una aproximación*

Hubo un hombre tan inteligente, que durante toda su vida amó a una sola mujer. Y su esposa jamás llegó a enterarse (58).

Para quitarse el complejo de Edipo, lo mejor es tener una madrastra (12).

La fidelidad masculina casi siempre suele ser consecuencia de tener mala suerte con las mujeres (77).

La bigamia es tener una mujer de más. Es decir, igual a la monogamia (206).

El matrimonio es como la historia de los países coloniales: primero viene la conquista y luego se sueña con la independencia (76).

Hay solteronas que lo son porque prefieren cien años de soledad a crimen y castigo (73).

Almazán, 1980

Si la mujer hasta ahora no se ha hecho visible, si responde a una imagen que le ha dictado la sociedad, la Iglesia, la familia, ¿cómo es posible que se manifieste a través de la escritura? (2).

Poniatowska, Agosto 1975

---

* This paper is a slightly modified version of one presented in the Primer Coloquio Fronterizo: Mujer y Literatura Mexicana y Chicana: Culturas en Contacto, April 1987, Tijuana, Baja California, Mexico. The author has since worked through many of the ideas here presented in summary form, and those wishing to pursue any aspect of this research, or share their own findings, are welcome to contact her directly: Peggy Job, S.L.A.S., University of N.S.W., P.O. Box 1, Kensington. 2033. AUSTRALIA.

Pienso que cuando una mujer se ha sentido afectada por vivir en una sociedad machista, es inevitable que esto se refleje en sus obras.

Rábago Palafox, 1981

En este panorama de la narrativa mexicana femenina, me propongo identificar unas características generales de la escritura respecto al tema de la sexualidad. El estudio, y sus conclusiones tentativas, forma parte de una investigación en desarrollo. No pretendo hacer una discusión teórica en este foro, sino invitarles a leer. En vez de analizar unos textos, lo juzgo más útil presentarles a las autoras siendo la mayoría de ellas apenas conocidas fuera y dentro de México. Por supuesto, existe mucha variación en oficio entre ellas, pero vale la pena enfatizar desde el principio, que en México escriben narradoras de calidad como Rosario Castellanos (quien ya reconocen, sin duda), Inés Arredondo, Julieta Campos, Luisa Josefina Hernández, Josefina Vicens, Elena Poniatowska, Aline Pettersson y María Luisa Puga, y otras de mucha promesa, como Gabriela Rábago Palafox, Mónica de Neymet y Ethel Krauze.

Aunque suele ser obvio, juzgo necesario empezar con unos rasgos de las escritoras y su contexto. Para escribir, y ser publicada, se supone una educación, una independencia económica, un espacio y un tiempo 'libre' adecuados para la producción del texto. Tratamos de un grupo privilegiado, dentro de un país transtornado por una crisis económica, y las obras reflejan el origen de sus autoras.[1]

Además, como dice un personaje de Rosario Castellanos:

En México, las alternativas y las circunstancias de las mujeres son muy limitadas y muy precisas. La que quiere ser algo más o algo menos que hija, esposa y madre, puede escoger entre convertirse en una oveja negra o en un chivo expiatorio; en una piedra de escándalo o de tropiezos; en un objeto de envidia o de irrisión. (*Album de familia*, 149)

Las dificultades para una artista en este país tan profundamente católico, con un concepto tradicional respecto a los papeles de mujer, se reflejan tanto en la baja producción de tantas escritoras, como en los textos mismos.[2]

Las alternativas, sin duda, son muy limitadas, y los círculos pequeños. Esther Seligson, aunque pretende decir otra cosa, afirma las contradicciones:

> En el fondo el mexicano es muy débil hacia el sexo femenino basta que sepas coquetear, basta que no seas demasiado fea, para que no te pongan obstáculos. Así que no creo que en México las mujeres que quieren publicar tengan ninguna dificultad por el hecho de ser mujeres. (1974)

No especifica la importancia del amiguismo, ni del patronazgo y caciquismo cultural que todavía influyen en la publicación, la crítica y el éxito de la escritura femenina.

La investigación presenta muchas dificultades en su desarrollo. Es sumamente difícil, en primer lugar, encontrar las obras. Los tirajes de una primera edición son entre 1,000 y 4,000 ejemplares, aun por una escritora con tres novelas publicadas. Pocas llegan a la suerte de ser re-editadas por la SEP (30,000 ejemplares), y la selección de estas parece bastante al azar.[3] La crítica tampoco es amplia; muchas veces las reseñas de los periódicos constituyen la única fuente de comentarios. Si apenas explicitan la sexualidad en las obras, mucho menos se trata el tema en la crítica. Encima de esto, siendo extranjera, la elección de un tema que toca a la intimidad de otra cultura, es atrevida. El proceso de hacer la investigación se parece al proceso de hacer el amor: a la vez que va desnudando y descubriendo las partes sensibles del cuerpo a su lado—sus pudores, sus prejuicios, sus profundidades—también va enfrentándose a los propios. Por bien y por mal, se termina por apasionarse del objeto del proceso, y el objetivismo asume su cara de angustia frente a las contradicciones experimentadas; la sensibilidad de la comprensión, en lugar de la cara fría de lo académico.

Una de las características más evidentes es la de la voz narrativa, en su mayoría femenina. Mientras la primera persona predomina, el uso de tercera persona omnisciente más comúnmente representa la perspectiva de la protagonista. Sin embargo, muchas autoras han mezclado sus voces narrativas, haciéndose así una obra más compleja estructuralmente. *Nostalgia de Troya* de Luisa Josefina Hernández, *Testimonios sobre Mariana* de Elena Garro, *Casi en silencio* de Aline Pettersson, y las obras de Carmen Rosezweig y Margo Glantz son unos ejemplos de este método. (See bibliography in this volume).

Las pocas novelas que emplean una voz narrativa masculina lo hacen con mucho éxito: *Los años falsos* (voz de adolescente), de Josefina Vicens es entre las mejores novelas que he leído; *Todo ángel es terrible* (voz de niño) de Gabriela Rábago Palafox es muy impresionante como primera novela, y la curiosa novela de Aline Pettersson, Proyectos de muerte (voz de adulto), rompe la idea de que su obra (5 novelas hasta ahora) trata exclusivamente de la mujer moderna.

Repecto a los cuentos, se encuentra más variación en la voz narrativa, incluso el uso de perspectivas masculinas. Por ejemplo unos cuentos de Inés Arredondo; el de Elena Poniatowska, "Métase mi prieta, entre el durmiente y el silbatazo" en *De noche vienes*, y el de Emma Dolujanoff, "La cuesta de las ballenas" en *Mujeres en espejo*.

La predominancia de la voz narrativa femenina invita la conclusión que muchos han notado, es decir, que la mayoría de la escritura femenina pretende narrar la experiencia específicamente femenina. No comparto la crítica (masculina, por lo general), que identifica a esta escritura como 'menor' en sí, aunque reconozca las dificultades que se presentan al analizar un texto donde la 'distancia' entre la escritura y la autora no está bien definida. Tampoco me subscribo a la noción de que cuando las escritoras sean 'grandes', con mayor oficio, etc., no van a escribir en el mismo estilo; sino afirmo que vayan a escribir, con sus elementos autobiográficos y todo, un libro tan distinguido como *Album de familia* de la todavía subestimada (¿por hacerla mito?) Rosario Castellanos.

Pero si las autoras recuerdan la experiencia femenina, ¿dónde está la sexualidad femenina? Son muy pocas las obras que se aproximan al tema explícita y/o abiertamente. La seducción de Ausencia (*De ausencia* de María Luisa Mendoza)—todo un éxito— estalla en el cuerpo de la narración de los 70 con su insípida fórmula de "qué felicidad".

Son muchas las explicaciones que se nos pueden ocurrir para este fenómeno tan significante. Una manera de percibirlo es como un aspecto de la opresión de la mujer en que "la sexualidad femenina se había cubierto de silencio y convertido en 'deber'; el embarazo y el parto, en dolor; la vagina y la regla, en basura y suciedad; el clitoris, en el órgano de fijación de las retrasadas mentales; la sensibilidad femenina, en la gigantesca máscara de la opresión y de la servidumbre" (Bradu, 1979: 32). A la vez podemos ir aun más allá, y afirmar que apenas se menciona el embarazo ni el parto, la vagina ni la regla, ni mucho menos el clitoris, es menester poner mucha atención a este 'silencio', porque está lleno de murmullos avergonzados subtextuales. Tantos textos huelen a una insatisfacción sexual por parte de las protagonistas, pero son pocas las que la admiten: la recién casada de "Lección de cocina" (*Album de familia* de Rosario Castellanos), la Jesusa indomable (*Hasta no verte, Jesús mío* de Elena Poniatowska), "La mula en la noria" de Ethel Krauze (*Intermedio para mujeres*).

Esta especie de pudor, que se observa tanto en la manera de escribir, como en las protagonistas, tenemos que considerarlo dentro del contexto de una ideología católica, en que los modelos de lo femenino son Eva y la Virgen María, modelos opuestos, y en que la forma mexicana proporciona a la Madre una mayúscula problemática. Es muy atrevida la escritora que desafía las opiniones o prejuicios de los maridos, los hijos, los padres, los tíos, los abuelos, los suegros—sobre todo, la suegra, siempre objeto de desprecio en la narrativa femenina—en una sociedad donde la familia tiene tanta importancia. Como indica María Luisa Puga, "Una escribe desde la noción de que hay muchas novelas cuyos autores se dijeron en un momento dado 'me voy a avergonzar de ella', y uno pone todos los medios para que esto no ocurra" (1978). La autocensura rige.

En cuanto a la 'sexualidad' femenina en este estudio, la narrativa en sí invita a una definición casi exclusivamente del acto sexual entre hembra y varón; se supone genital en la ausencia de mencionar otras alternativas. En el único ejemplo de sexo oral que he encontrado hasta ahora, "la multitud se precipitó sobre ellos con piedras y palos"... bueno, es una novela 'bíblica' (Seligson, 1981: 22). Es interesante que las obras que mencionan explícitamente el lesbianismo y la masturbación, han salido a partir de 1985. Se supone que unos de los factores ya mencionados sean responsables por esta situación, y no que las mexicanas acabaron de descubrir estas formas de sexualidad. Aunque Alicia es suficientemente moderna para *hablar* abiertamente de la masturbación (*Los limones*, de Olga Harmony), lo *hacen* sólamente Livia, con vergüenza (*El bien y el mal* de Manú Dornbierer), Adelina (*Sombra ella misma* de Aline Pettersson), y Catalina. Es posible que la popularidad de *Arráncame la vida* de Angeles Mastretta se deba en parte a la frescura de esta heroína, cuyos experimentos con su propio cuerpo despiertan a toda su casa.

Aunque una pueda sospechar de la vida personal de tantas tías (solteronas y medias raras) que pueblan los mundos creativos de Beatriz Espejo (*Muros de azogue*), Adela Fernández (*Duermevelas*) o Bárbara Jacobs (*Doce cuentos en contra*), es la siempre atrevida China Mendoza la que hace explícita la relación sexual entre mujeres ("¿Por qué fue a Chalma el Marqués?" en *Ojos de papel volando*). Otras autoras consideran el tema de la homosexualidad entre hombres: Seligson brevemente en la obra ya citada, Elena Garro con insistencia en *Reencuentro de personajes*, Aline Pettersson describe una relación triángular amorosa que incluye a dos hombres (*Casi en silencio*) Rábago Palafox explora la 'etapa adolescente', y Castellanos y Arredondo tocan el tema. La impresión que se da, entonces, es que o la homosexualidad es más común que el lesbianismo o que es más fácil escribir sobre ella.

Esta falta de exploración de las varias formas de expresión sexual de la mujer en la narrativa, se repite en un silencio curioso en relación a todos los aspectos del cuerpo, que hace de una mujer un ser asexuado. Muy pocas protagonistas tienen la menstruación, y no más de una vez; por supuesto, nadie sufre de tensión premenstrual. El parto, como experiencia, se pasa por arriba; se quedan los hijos ya hechos, y una de las más profundas exploraciones de su ser como mujer no vale la pena mencionar. ¿Amamantan? Con pocas excepciones, la maternidad es la que experimenta su propia madre, y no sí misma; *nadie* goza de ella, que me parece sumamente raro en esta cultura del culto a la Madre. El aborto nadie lo tiene, salvo una por accidente; tampoco es tema de discusión. ¿Los anticonceptivos existen? ¿funcionan? ¿influyen en el acto? ¿dan asco? La menopausia es una acusación (*Álbum de familia*) o una broma (*Los limones*); la vejez siempre se puede borrar con el suicidio (*Sombra ella misma*).

Es como si fuera el cuerpo de la mujer una abstracción, ajena a la persona; o más bien, el reflejo en el espejo que tanto mira. Respecto a la experiencia sexual explícita, la desfloración es descrita pocas veces, y casi todas son violaciones, aunque dentro del matrimonio: Delfina Careaga describe la violación de una sirvienta de 11 años en "Rezo" (*Cosas del tiempo y otros fantasmas*); Livia (*El bien y el mal*) y la señora Justina (*Álbum de familia*) están avergonzadas y horrorizadas por sus maridos ineptos; Adelina descubre sus propias profundidades en su única relación con Felipe en un tren (*Sombra ella misma*), y Ausencia está encantada por la experiencia (*De ausencia*). Alicia busca su desfloración como una manera de afirmar y asumir su propia sexualidad, con consecuencias horrendas cuando es descubierta (*Los limones*). En cuanto al orgasmo, tenemos que contentarnos con "soy la mujer más feliz del mundo" (Molina, 1977: 13) o creemos, con Jesusa, que tiene tan poca importancia que "El tenía con qué y lo hacía y ya" (Poniatowska, 1969: 86). Ni se imaginan los orgasmos múltiples; mucho menos las múltiples maneras de llegar a esta 'felicidad'.

Felicitamos a Mendoza y a Fernández por hacer explícito el incesto que permea tantas obras, a través de las relaciones peculiares entre padre e hija, entre hermanos, entre primos y sobre todo, entre madre e hijo. Todavía no tenemos un Bataille[4] entre nuestras autoras, pero Vicens se acerca al problema sin nombre en su texto, cuando Luis Alfonso hace el amor con la amante de su padre (*Los años falsos*).

Mientras podemos disfrutar de la ironía de Castellanos o Margo Glantz, la intelectualización de Seligson, o el goce tan aparente de Mastretta y Mendoza, el tono que se adopta en la narrativa al aproximarse a la relación sexual es casi siempre serio. ¿Dónde están las risas que deben acompañar este acto humano tan intrínsicamente ridículo?

Lo que me ha sido doloroso y chocante descubrir es la misoginia que impregna la narrativa. Incluye la estereotipización de la mujer según los modelos de los hombres, y una actitud de menosprecio frente a las demás mujeres por parte de la narradora y/o protagonista femenina. Se puede argumentar (como lo ha hecho Krauze) que esto refleja la 'realidad' de la sociedad de la cual el texto trata, o en la cual se han formado las autoras; pero si comparamos estos textos con los que han salido en otros países durante la misma época, el contraste es brutal. La celebración de la amistad-solidaridad femeninas, que tanto ha sido tema de la escritura femenina en Europa, los EE.UU. o Australia durante los 70, está ausente en la narrativa mexicana, tanto como exploración de la relación madre-hija en búsqueda de una comprensión mutua de generaciones de mujeres. Quizás esta misoginia llegue a su cumbre en el retrato de la Premio Nobel de *Donde las cosas vuelen*, aun cuando Ethel Krauze es una escritora de la nueva generación; pero la misoginia está presente en tantos textos que una se deprime.

María Luisa Puga explora la misoginia a través de su narradora en *Pánico o peligro*, y su relación con Socorro, la amiga hermosa que se acuesta con muchos hombres. Susana puede 'entender' a Socorro sólo cuando descubre que lo hace por la revolución. Este es uno de los pocos textos donde tenemos la posibilidad de ver las relaciones entre mujeres a un nivel más o menos íntimo y a través de un largo tiempo; el período que atraviesa la niñez, la adolescencia y la madurez. Esta transición es importante, porque dentro de una sociedad heterosexual (y sexista), la mujer pasa desde la identificación con otras mujeres (niñas) a una identificación con un(os) hombre(s). Mientras existen en la narrativa muchos ejemplos de la amistad, o aun colusión, entre niñas o muchachas, en el momento en que aparece El Hombre, la amiga está abandonada; desaparece de la vida 'principal' de la protagonista. Bárbara Jacobs lo describe en "La vez que me emborraché" (*Doce cuentos en contra*), Pettersson en *Círculos*, Dornbierer en *El bien y el mal*, Harmony en *Los limones* (muy, pero muy explícitamente), y Oralba Castillo Nájera en "Querido Melchor" (*Sin Permiso*).

No nos sorprende, entonces, que tanta narrativa sobre los años mayores grite la soledad, o el sentido de desamparo. Las mujeres de *Album de familia*, "En la sombra" (*Río subterráneo* de Arredondo), *El aullido crepitante de una dama nostálgica* de Miriam Ruvinskis, "La casita de sololoi" (*De noche vienes* de Poniatowska), varios cuentos de la colección *Sin Permiso*, y tantos textos más, expresan aspectos de este desamparo y soledad.

Esta identificación exclusiva con un hombre, y la consiguiente aislación de la mujer, tanto física como emocional, sirve muy bien al patriarcado y al sistema de clases: así la mujer siente sus frustraciones y problemas como individuo, y no como una parte de una colectividad que puede organizarse y luchar.

Como parte de una misoginia, vale la pena examinar la relación madre-hija. Por lo general, la perspectiva que tenemos es la de la hija, y demuestra una relación conflictiva, de poca comprensión mutua. Cuando tenemos la oportunidad de verla desde la perspectiva de la madre nos encontramos una competencia, envidia, y desprecio profundo: "Cabecita blanca" (*Album de familia*) y el realmente horroroso cuento de Krauze, "Rumbo al Popo" (*Intermedio para mujeres*). Curioso también, es el hecho de que en muchos textos la madre es una figura en la sombra, aparte; a veces perdida en la locura o en una enfermedad; en el suicidio o en la muerte temprana. Juana Armanda Alegría en *Diálogo prohibido* (título deliberadamente elegido), ha especificado el odio entre madre e hija, por el hecho de no haber nacido varón, y las consecuencias horrendas para la niñez y la adolescencia de la hija.

Otra vez, nos enfrentamos a una identificación con un hombre;

el padre, a fuerzas, en este caso. Mientras sea fácil elaborar una hipótesis psicológica-freudiana respecto a esta situación, me parece insuficiente como técnica de análisis de textos que han surgido de una cultura profundamente católica y patriarcal.

Por eso, en este momento, prefiero sugerir unas explicaciones tentativas para la manera de escribir, basadas en la cultura de las autoras. Las características identificadas invitan a este punto de partida: La voz narrativa es de mujer, principalmente, pero la sexualidad femenina se queda en la sombra del sobrentendido; el disfrute y plena experiencia del cuerpo de mujer en todos sus aspectos, apenas se tratan, y cuando lo hace, es como una abstracción o vergüenza; el tono de escribir de la sexualidad es serio, aproximándose a lo sagrado, como si se acercara a Dios; la mujer está sola, no se alinea con otras mujeres para compartir experiencias ni angustias: compiten y se menosprecian. Todos parecen aspectos de un profundo desprecio de sí misma por parte de la narradora o mujer protagónica.

Si la sexualidad femenina se expresa en relaciones heterosexuales, estamos metidas en la relación hombre-mujer, que al nivel estructural en la sociedad, es una relación de poder. Tomás Segovia dijo, "La mujer . . . es la única clase que hace el amor con su opresor." (Urrutia, 1975: 7) Mientras no considere a las mujeres como una clase, lo que Segovia está indicando es la semejanza (o igualdad) entre relaciones de clases y relaciones patriarcales: en los dos casos un grupo tiene poder sobre otro grupo. La omnipresente y abrumadora naturaleza de la ideología sexista puede terminar por convencernos de su 'normalidad' su 'naturalidad', hasta tal punto que estamos incapacitadas para hacer la crítica, mucho menos para romper las restricciones que insisten que 'la mujer no habla de estas cosas'. No nos tienen que censurar; lo hacemos nosotras.

De acuerdo con Anais Nin, ". . . El hecho de que las mujeres escriben sobre sexualidad no significa su liberación . . . " (citada en Batis, 1984: 110), pero el no escribir sobre un aspecto tan fundamental de la vida del ser humano, surgiere una falta de conciencia política sorprendente en la Década de la Mujer. Tanto me gustaría ponerme de acuerdo con Julieta Campos cuando dice, ". . . la diferencia entre una prosa 'masculina' y una prosa 'femenina' ¿será entonces que esa que quiero llamar 'femenina' es una escritura que abandona todos los apoyos sólidos para deslizarse hacia zonas prohibidas, hacia ámbitos nocturnos, hacia la experiencia de lo innombrable..." (Campos, Agosto 1978), pero a pesar de las excepciones, la escritura femenina mexicana no demuestra tal abandono.[5]

No quiere decir que las narradoras mexicanas carezcan de conciencia política, o por lo menos, de una crítica social. Esto lo podemos observar en la obra de varias: Arredondo, Poniatowska, Puga, Puglia, Solis, Harmony, entre otras, a través de su preocupación en los problemas de clases, de racismo, de los marginados, de la represión. Pero es poco común la confrontación explícita y directa al patriarcado, y sus consecuencias espantosas.

Una lectura superficial de la narrativa femenina corre el riesgo de dejarnos creyendo que la violencia inherente en la relación entre seres desiguales, entre hombres y mujeres, sólo sucede en el Otro México de los pobres de Cristina Pacheco. Sus cuentos "Padre, he aquí a tu hijo" (*Sopita de fideos*) y "Ceremonia secreta" (*Para vivir aquí*), son ejemplos de muchos en donde ella hace explícitas las relaciones de familia que se quedan escondidas o implícitas en otras obras.

Puede ser precisamente por la razón de escribir dentro de una sociedad sexista, que la sexualidad es discutida subtextualmente. Es decir, las tácticas para enfrentar el problema de la relación hombre-mujer en una situación de desigualdad que emplean las mujeres para ganarse un espacio—la persuación, la sutileza, la manipulación, la ironía, el socavar desde abajo, la fachada de sumisión, la 'gigantesca máscara' en fin—son las que aparecen en la narrativa. Como dice Rosario Castellanos, "Se han acusado a las mujeres de hipócritas y la acusación no es infundada. Pero la hipocresía es la respuesta que a sus opresores da el oprimido, que a los fuertes contestan los débiles, que los subordinados devuelven al amo. La hipocresía es... un reflejo condicionado de defensa... cuando los peligros son muchos y las opciones son pocas." (1973: 25)

Considerando la obra narrativa durante el período 1970-1987, tenemos que ponernos de acuerdo con Poniatowska en su juicio—desde hace más de diez años—y afirmar que "... ninguna de las escritoras mencionadas da la impresión de haber escrito acerca de lo que realmente la conmueve, sus fantasías sexuales... sus sentimientos violentos en contra de su madre o en contra del hombre..." (octubre 1975e:4), a la vez que expresamos cierto optimismo, exactamente en la definición que hace Poniatowska.

Durante los años más recientes, a partir de 1983-84 más o

menos, podemos ver un cambio en unas de estas características. Mientras la conciencia feminista notada en el desarrollo de escritoras españolas (Zatlin, 1987) todavía no es una tendencia clara en la narrativa mexicana, ni podemos incluir a las escritoras mexicanas en el tipo de análisis optimista hecho por Bassnett sobre Latinoamérica (1987), o de Welles sobre escritoras chilenas y argentinas (1983), hay indicios del principio de unos cambios profundos. Tres novelas indican un cambio lento en las relaciones entre mujeres, por ejemplo.

La buena novela *Los limones* (1984), demuestra todos los conflictos de la mujer rebelde, inteligente, que quiere afirmarse como persona íntegra. Describe los obstáculos en una cultura sexista-católica: la familia, el novio y su madre, las amigas; reconoce la trampa del hombre bueno-solidario, y se queda sola con la única salida: intenta el suicidio. La tragedia es individual, experimentada por Alicia como individuo; el texto no le permite el apoyo de otras mujeres, sino al contrario, una condena absoluta.

Pánico o peligro (1983) rastrea cierta toma de conciencia por parte de la narradora,[6] Susana—aunque hace sufrir a la lectora su lentitud pasmada—pero curiosamente, este proceso depende mucho en la influencia de los hombres en su vida. Aunque Lourdes es su amiga íntima, no existen indicios textuales de una discusión entre las dos de lo que toca a sus intimidades como mujeres, sino una reticencia profunda.[7]

En *El bien y el mal* (1986), aunque una novela con fallas, observamos ciertos cambios fundamentales. La vida de Livia sigue la trayectoria 'normal': adolescencia sana e inocente, matrimonio temprano y traumático, nacimiento de hijos queridos, y por fin, un amante experto. En vez de quedarse allá, decide dejar al matrimonio y dos de sus hijos, y al amante y volver a estudiar, empezar de nuevo su vida. La toma de conciencia es fuerte y angustiada, pero ella se hace sujeto en vez de objeto. Además, las decisiones de Livia dependen fundamentalmente de la comprensión y apoyo de sus dos amigas y de su hermana, demostrando así los principios de una solidaridad entre mujeres.

Mientras damos la bienvenida a la aparición de protagonistas femeninas 'modernas', como Livia, y más reciente en las novelas *Las horas vivas* de Mónica de Neymet, y *Las líneas de la mano* de Hortensia Moreno, o en cuentos como los de *Mala memoria* de Mónica Mansour, son protagonistas todavía angustiadas. Aunque Catalina sea una mujer simpática, ha aceptado la corrupción y el ejercicio desapiadado del poder de su marido, incluso el asesinato de su amado-amante; es una mujer que al fin y al cabo, se vende; su *joie de vivre,* una ilusión.

Pero dentro de la angustia, también hay cambios. Unas escritoras están re-escribiendo los mitos, tomándolos como suyos, escribiendo desde su cuerpo de mujer. Magaly Martínez Gamba y Esther Seligson lo han hecho, y Angelina Muñiz presenta dos versiones de mitos sumamente interesantes en *Huerto cerrado, huerto sellado* (1985): "Yocasta confiesa" reescribe el mito de Edipo, y "La ofrenda más grata" el de Caín y Abel con una 'Caína'.

Tal vez más interesante todavía es el tratamiento de las relaciones sexuales entre mujeres, descritas en dos novelas recientes: *Sed de mar* (1986), de Seligson, y *Los colores ocultos* (1986) de Pettersson. Curiosamente, las descripciones coinciden de una manera extraordinaria, incluso en el uso de imágenes y lenguaje. Más que esto, en cada caso, el hacer el amor con otra mujer simboliza el descubrimiento de su ser, por parte de la protagonista; una manera de llegar a su propio cuerpo de la Otra, un espejo de sí misma que ya no refleja su imagen. Apenas ha empezado el viaje en la narrativa en que la mujer-protagonista se hace sujeto en vez de 'paisaje' (Monsiváis, en Urrutia, 1975: 107), pero está en marcha.

Esperamos, todavía, una heroína de la narrativa femenina mexicana que desafíe el orden establecido, que triunfe en su lucha para asumir su propia identidad, que celebre su cuerpo y sexualidad femeninos, que diga orgullosamente, sonriendo: a la chingada con todos; aquí soy yo.

Notas:

1. Casi todas las obras ubican a sus protagonistas dentro de la clase media o la burguesía. Mientras unas obras incluyen a personajes de la clase trabajadora (sirvientas, sobre todo, pero también campesinos), son pocas las que hacen protagonistas principales de este grupo. La versátil Elena Poniatowska es una excepción; tiene la facilidad de escribir la perspectiva de los marginados, tanto como la de los burgueses. Aun cuando no se considera entre las mejores escritoras, hay que destacar a Cristina Pacheco. Ella escribe cuentos cortos, casi todos relacionados con los marginados, los campesinos o la clase trabajadora urbana, es decir, el Otro México. Es autora comprometida que quiere describir un ambiente lejos de las preocupaciones usuales en la narrativa femenina: atestigua a la

violencia, las violaciones, un catolicismo fuerte y complejo, creencias y prejuicios implacables, el sufrimiento diario e inescapable de los de abajo. No teme al desafío directo: se atreve a nombrar tanto la corrupción como el patriarcado, y contar sus consecuencias.
2. Sefchovich (1983) discute estos temas más ampliamente en su introducción a los cuentos de autoras latinoamericanas.
3. El estudio de Brushwood (1984) de la novela mexicana 1967-82, cita a 22 novelas de escritoras entre más de 200 novelas citadas—es decir el 10% de siempre. La SEP (Secretaría de Educación Pública) sigue la misma fórmula.
4. Véase *Mi madre* de Georges Bataille (ed. en español, Premiá, 1979).
5. Para una discusión más amplia de la 'escritura femenina', véanse *fem.* III:10 (1979) y IV:21 (1982).
6. Notada por López González, 1987.
7. Más bien esto indica más sobre el estilo de la autora; parece más cómoda en su exploración del psique masculino. Véase *Cuando el aire es azul.*

Referencias:

Almazán, Marco A. *Píldoras anticonceptivas.* México: Editorial Diana, 1980.
Bassnett, Susan. "Coming Out of the Labyrinth: Women Writers in Contemporary Latin America," in *Modern Latin American Fiction: A Survey,* John King (ed). London: Faber and Faber, 1987, 264-267.
Batis, Humberto. *Estética de lo obsceno.* México: UAEM, 1984.
Bradu, Fabienne. "Sobre la literatura feminista en Francia." *fem* III:10 (1979), 31-33.
Brushwood, John S. *La novela mexicana (1967-1982).* México: Grijalbo, 1984.
Campos, Julieta. "¿Tiene sexo la escritura?" *Vuelta* 21 (Agosto 1978).
Castellanos, Rosario. *Album de la familia.* México: Joaquín Mortiz, 1971.
_____. *Mujer que sabe latín. . . .* México: SepSetentas, 1973.
López González, Aralia. "Una literatura de la diferencia," ponencia presentada en el Coloquio del PIEM, El Colegio de México, 10 de marzo, 1987.
Molina, Sylvia. *La mañana debe ser gris.* México: Joaquín Mortiz, 1977.
Poniatowska, Elena. "Las escritoras mexicanas calzan zapatos que les aprietan." *Los universitarios* 54-55 (15-31 agosto 1975), 2-3.
_____. "Sólo hay doce novelistas mexicanas y de ellas sólo cuatro cuentan con más de dos novelas." *Los universitarios* 58-59 (15-31 octubre 1975), 2-4.
_____. *Hasta no verte, Jesús mío.* México: ERA 1969.
Prieto, Guillermo. "Alma: El Caballo del diablo." *fem* III:10 (1979), 44-48.

Puga, María Luisa. "Entrevista con Elena Urrutia." *Uno más uno*, 7/X/78.
Rábago Palafox, Gabriela. Entrevistada por Gustavo Masso, en *El universal*, 24/VIII/81.
Sefchovich, Sara, ed. *Mujeres en espejo 1*. México: Folios Edic., 1983.
Seligson, Esther. *La Morada en el Tiempo*. México: Artífice, 1981.
_____. Entrevista con Beth Miller, en *Los universitarios*, 38-39 (15-31 diciembre 1974).
Urrutia, Elena, ed. *Imagen y realidad de la mujer*. México: SepSetentas, 1975.
Welles, Marcia L. "The Changing Face of Woman in Latin American Fiction." In *Women in Hispanic Literature: Icons and Fallen Idols*, Miller, Beth, ed. Berkeley: University of California Press, 1983.
Zatlin, Phyllis. "Women Novelists in Democratic Spain: Freedom to Express the Female Perspective." In *Anales de la Literatura Española Contemporánea*, 12: 1-2 (1987), 29-44.

Juanita Luna Lawhn

El Regidor and *La Prensa:* Impediments to Women's Self–definition

Recent historical literary studies are documenting and illustrating the influence of Spanish-language newspapers on contemporary Chicano literature.[1] These studies illustrate that Chicano literature is a natural outgrowth and a continuation of an on-going Hispanic literary tradition that has always been present in the United States, especially in the Southwest and in the greater Chicago area. Consequently, the theory often vocalized that today's Chicano literary as well as non-literary community has evolved strictly from an oral tradition is no longer viable.[2] Instead, a new theory which states that the literary, social, and moral development of the Chicano community has been strongly influenced by the written word can and should modify and redefine the old theory of orality.

Documentation of the tremendous influence of Spanish language newspapers on the Chicano community is worthy of admiration and pride for the small group of Chicano scholars who are attempting to recreate and document Chicano literary history in a country that values the written word as a vehicle for its moral development. For women, however, especially feminists, it is a statement of great concern, a concern that originates from the knowledge that during the first half of the twentieth century, the editorial staff of most Spanish languages newspapers in the United States was predominately male and followed an unquestioned patriarchal model of morality. Consequently, the morality of the Chicano community, particularly the morality of women, was molded, controlled and manipulated by the male-dominated press. While there were as many as twenty-nine Spanish language newspapers printed daily, weekly, or monthly in San Antonio in the late 1800's and the beginning of the 1900's ("Más de cuatrocientos periódicos...," 7), I will utilize *El Regidor* and *La*

Prensa to illustrate that the morality disseminated by these two newspapers impeded the development of the Mexican woman because it prohibited her from questioning the social order. *El Regidor,* founded and edited by Pablo Cruz and his brother, Victor Cruz, was printed from 1888 to 1914 ("Rasgos biográficos...," i); *La Prensa,* owned and edited by Ignacio E. Lozano, was published from February 13, 1913, to May, 1959. Though *La Prensa* followed *El Regidor* in publication history both had much in common. First, both papers were founded by individuals who left Mexico to make their living in the U.S. In 1877, Mr. Abraham Cruz Valdéz and Mrs. Vivian Cárdenas de Cruz brought their eleven-year-old son, Pablo, to the United States ("Rasgos biográficos...," i); Ignacio E. Lozano came to the United States during the Mexican Revolution of 1910. Both papers viewed European culture as the model to emulate. Cognizant of the French presence in Mexican culture, both papers reinforced and reaffirmed French influence by printing translations of major French writers such as Alexander Dumas and Victor Hugo. Furthermore, *La Prensa* presented France as the arbiter of high culture. Moreover, both papers felt a strong responsibility to guide the moral and intellectual development of their Mexican constituency. The policy is clearly stated in the biographical sketch of Pablo Cruz written soon after his death:

> Fundó este semanario bajo el nombre que aun conserva, *El Regidor,* publicándose desde el principio en idioma español y adoptando como meta principal la defensa de los intereses de los individuos de su raza y el adelantamiento moral, físico e intelectual de los mismos ("Rasgos biográficos...," i).

Known as the educator of *El Méxicano de Afuera*—the generation of Mexican exiles who were forced to leave Mexico because of the Mexican Revolution of 1910—Ignacio E. Lozano accepted the responsibility of educating the Mexican community of San Antonio, the Southwest, and Europe ("Lozano, un educador...,"[8]). Consequently, the ideology of *El México de Afuera,* an ideogogy based on a strong nationalism, Catholicism, and wealth becomes the ideology that is disseminated throughout the Southwest, Mexico, and Europe.

Because both papers viewed themselves as responsible for the moral, intellectual, and spiritual development of its reading public, especially the moral development of women, both papers published regularly the accepted code of behavior for the "ideal" or "modern" Mexican woman. For example, the item "Los mandamientos" printed on August 27, 1896, is representative of the moral code that was consistently disseminated by *El Regidor*. Furthermore, by attributing the code to an unnamed English woman, the newspaper acknowledges its acceptance of Angloeuropean models for its societal behavior. Consequently, the item implies that if a woman were to earn a place in an elite society, the "good" or the "ideal" Mexican woman should conform, adapt, and accept Europe's fashionable behavior. In the article, "Los mandamientos" the code of behavior of a "good" wife is enumerated as follows:

1. Guárdate de la primera querella, pero una vez empezada, no la evites, arréglate de manera de vencer a tú marido y que lo reconozca;
2. No olvides que te has casado con un hombre y no con un Dios, no te extrañes de sus imperfecciones y defectos;
3. No lo atropelles exigiéndole dinero, trata de arreglarte con las sumas que te ha fijado;
4. Es posible que tu marido no tenga corazón, pero posible en confeccionarte una cocina excelente;
5. Dale la razón de tiempo en tiempo, pero no muy a menudo, eso lo agradara y no te causara ningun perjucio;
6. Lee en los periódicos otra cosa que no sean las noticias de matrimonio y difunciones, a fin de que puedas hablar en ciertos casos algo que le interese;
7. Sé siempre complaciente con él, acuérdate que cuando era tu prometido tú no lo despreciabas como un ser inferior a ti;
8. Déjalo creer algunas veces que él sabe más que tú, eso lo agasajará;
9. Sé para él una amiga si es inteligente, trata de elevarle a tú altura si es ignorante;
10. Respeta a sus padres, sobre todo a su madre, que quiso antes que a ti. (2)

A "good" woman is encouraged to sacrifice and devote her entire life to her husband. In every case, she must renounce her wishes and desires in order that her husband may be able to perceive himself as superior; however, even though she must prostitute herself and fulfill the role of a prostitute by decorating herself to please and seduce her husband, she does not have the right to charge for her services. The code clearly states, "No lo atropelles exigiéndole dinero, trata de arreglarte con las sumas que te ha fijado" (2). Furthermore, while the standards of a "good" woman are the epitome of perfection, the code justifies men's foibles by denying his "godliness," a contradiction that is evident within the same code since the behavior expected of women clearly illustrates that the man should be viewed as a superior Being, a "God." Since the code required that a woman relinquish her own economic, physical, and emotional needs, as well as her intelligence for the benefit of her husband, it kept her in a subordinate position thus restricting her potential for leadership, independence and initiative. Morever, implicitly, the code kept her from developing other social relations.

In the same way as *El Regidor*, *La Prensa* also published the acceptable code of behavior of the "good" wife and mother. Since the editorial staff of *La Prensa* was predominately male, the morality of women continues to be created, controlled, and manipulated by the male-dominated press. For example, the item entitled, "Código de las mujeres" (7) published in *La Prensa* on February 16, 1928, and reprinted on March 21, 1928, reiterates and reaffirms the limitations and boundaries of the moral behavior that had been printed earlier in *El Regidor*. According to *La Prensa*, the limitations of the modern Mexican woman were as follows:

1. No te esfuerces en tener muchas amigas. Hay una amiga desinteresada y noble: la madre;
2. Si tienes la felicidad de encontrar una amiga que siempre te aconseje bien, consérvala a todo trance;
3. Nunca seas ingrata con los que te han servido. La ingratitud mata todos los afectos;
4. Nunca te escudes en tu debilidad. La más triste de todas las debilidades es ser débil;
5. No busques en los hombres aquello que pasa fugazmente. Aprécialos más que por su dinero, por su caballerosidad y sus bondades;
6. Si quieres ser buena, huye de las malas mujeres;
7. Trabaja, porque el trabajo engrandece, dignifica y desaloja los malos deseos;
8. Viste con descencia. Desecha el lujo, porque éste es la causa de muchos males y de constantes humillaciones;
9. Aspira siempre a subir y ten mucho cuidado en no descender. El lodo cubre los diamantes; la luz abrillanta el carbón;
10. Sé como madre, amante, como hija, humilde, como esposa, amante y humilde, sé verdadera compañera del hombre elegido (7).

While the preceding code demonstrates that the behavioral

expectations of women printed in *La Prensa* were very similar to those of *El Regidor*, it also demonstrates that *La Prensa* defined moral conduct very specifically. For example, a moral woman did not exhibit ungrateful behavior, was not weak, that is she did not disobey the moral code, and she did not permit her sexual desires to get the best of her. In this way could she then be a strong woman. She dressed modestly, evaded the "bad" woman, and all costs, attempted to reach the apex of goodness. The implication is that obedience to the code would guarantee her her rightful place and honor in society.

While I have given only one example that illustrates the moral behavior of a "good" woman, there were many other articles printed that develop the same or similar themes. Futhermore, moral behavior was presented in binary terms; it was either good or bad. A woman could fall from good to evil, but, once she was evil or bad, she could never be good again. As the code states, "Aspira siempre a subir y ten mucho cuidado en no descender. El lodo cubre los diamantes; la luz abrillanta el carbón" (7).

On September 21, 1895, *El Regidor* printed an article titled, "Educad a la mujer" (3). While my first reaction to the title was of great joy, as I read the entire article, I realized that my definition of the term "Educad" was based on my expectations as a feminist and that I had lost my historical perspective. Yes, the paper was encouraging that the woman be educated, but her education was to be measured against a male measuring stick. It stated that it was important to educate a woman because an educated woman was beneficial to society since her primary role was that of a mother and a loyal campanion to man. As I continued to read the article, I was further devastated by the fact that the woman's education was to be restricted to the home and the mother was to assume the responsibility of being the first teacher. The article states, "¿Sabéis cual es la primera fuente de educación para la mujer? Es el hogar. ¿El primer maestro? La madre" (3).

The article continues as follows:

> Eduquemos a la mujer, a la fiel compañera del hombre en el páramo de la vida. Diremos al hombre con grito arrancado del alma: educad a la mujer, comparte con ella el pan intelectual y la labor de mañana se dividirá en dos partes. ¡Ah! que triste es la mujer sin educación; pues se parece a la

planta, que nacida en el desierto, está falta de agua que bañe sus raíces (3).

While the article states that Mothers are the first teachers of children, and the reader may assume that children's education is primarily carried out by women, further reading illustrates that the article continues to advocate the superiority of men. This is evident by the fact that even though the Mother is a child's first teacher, she, herself, has been already trained by a teacher superior to herself, a man. Consequently her teaching contains no individual originality but has been *a priori* defined by a code which has been controlled and manipulated by the male-dominated press. As a result when she assumes her position as Mother and Teacher, she propagates a morality which excludes her own vision of the social and moral order.

Because *El Regidor* views the responsibility of educating woman seriously, it sets out to accomplish its mission, for a paper that fails in its objective, fails humanity. This is evident in the following statement:

> Quien haya contemplado una planta falta de algo que constituya un elemento para su desarrollo, habrá visto en sus ramas, hojas que carecen de verdura, así mismo una madre falta de educación (en sentido moral) producirá hijos a quien no adoran ningunas virtudes (3).

Since woman is viewed as responsible for humanity, given her maternal role, she must be educated, but her education is beyond her control or choice; consequently, she is left without an alternative, but to become another vechicle that the press uses to disseminate the morality that it wishes to cultivate and encourage.

If a woman by chance should question the moral philosophy that she is decoding from the newspapers, her questioning will inevitably lead her to question her womanhood, for a "good woman" would accept her subservient position passively and appreciate her role as nurturer, companion, and mother. Thus if she questions the social behavior encouraged by the newspapers, she must not be a woman—She must not be "La verdadera mujer" (7). Since the newpapers are already defining the term "woman" for her, not to comply is tantamount to not being a woman and/or negating the "destiny" of her sex. This conflict is further complicated by the fact that she has been elevated to a "goddess" position, but a position defined by men. She has been placed on a pedestal, and once she has been anointed to that superior position, she has also been endowed with the responsibility of maintaining her position untainted. It is this reponsibility that has been imposed upon her that prohibits her from attaining a higher level of moral development by envisioning a different social order. The article titled "Virtud" printed in *El Regidor* on July 7, 1896 (2), is an example of the process of controlling women's moral behavior by elevating them to a position of moral excellence. The article states:

> La virtud es tan natural a la mujer como a la flor el aroma, como a la fuente el rumor, como a la miel la dulzura.
> La virtud debe ser la inseparable compañera de la mujer y la que dé el mayor realce a sus nobles cualidades.
> Angel mortal se llama y con razón a la mujer virtuosa; pues ella vela al lado de nuestra cuna y despues guía nuestros pasos, cuidando de nuestra dicha y nuestro bienestar. Es el ángel bendito que llaman madre.
> Inflamando su corazón con el fuego de la caridad, vuela a dar socorro al desvalido y pan al hambriento, ofreciendo muchas veces hasta el sacrificio de su vida por bien de sus hermanos, es entonces un ángel en forma humana a quien llaman la HERMANA DE LA CARIDAD. En el hogar, al lado de su esposo, llenando de caricias al hijo querido de su corazón y formando las delicias del hogar, es el ángel de tangible forma que llaman esposa....(2)

From a feminist point of view, this essay needs little explanation since Sandra M. Gilbert and Susan Gubar have done an excellent study of the Victorian woman as "Angel" myth. What is important is to note that the article clearly states that virtue is *inherent* in women and that God has endowed her with a responsibility to humanity. It states "La mujer ha recibido de Dios la misión de cultivar el campo de la vida, hermoseando con las flores de las virtudes" (2). Consequently, if God endowed her with the characteristic of virtue to be used for the benefit of others, such as her children and, especially her husband, how can she possibly act against what the code demands. And, since virtue is inherent in women, those women who do not display virtuous behavior are women that either God has chosen to exclude from His domain of "good" women or who have willfully gone against their "nature", thus becoming "monsters" of nature. It can be inferred that a woman who acts against the moral code disseminated by the newspapers would be classified as a deviant, a person behaving sacrilegiously. Furthermore, the code implies that not only would she be ostracized from the social community, but also from the Church. It is evident that the newspaper editors utilize terminology used within the Church, specificially the Catholic Church, to relate their message and to give credibility to the "truths" presented by the code. Breaking away from the code that is disseminated by the Spanish-language newspapers is actually viewed by society as breaking away from the Catholic Church. For a woman who has grown up in a strict Catholic community such as the community that represents and controls the Spanish-language newspapers in San Antonio, the threat of being ostracized from the Catholic Church is to be ostracized from her community—a high price to pay. Consequently, the moral behavior disseminated by *El Regidor* and *La Prensa* prohibits a woman from pursuing alternatives where she would be in control of making choices and of taking and accepting the responsibility for the consequences of her own actions, her own decisions, her own choices. It is this type of strict censorship that impedes an alternate moral development for women, in this case, the Mexiana/Chicana woman reading the Spanish-language newspapers in San Antonio, Texas.

Because the printed word is so permanent, because the distribution of both papers reached the Mexican reading public for whom it was intended, and because *La Prensa* attained the status of an "institution," the objective of both papers to control and create a morality for women could not have been anything else but successful, a success that unfortunately was not in the best interest of Chicanas.

Notes

1. See Juan Bruce-Novoa, "Estudio Introductorio" to Martin Luis Guzmán's *La Sombra del Caudillo: Versión Periodística.* México: UNAM, 1987; and Francisco Lomelí, "Eusebio Chacón: A Literary Profile of 19th Century New Mexico." Monograph of the Southwest Hispanic Research Institute, 1987.

2. See Marcienne Rocard, "The Chicano: A Minority in Search of a Proper Literary Medium for Self- Affirmation." In *Missions in Conflict: Essays on U.S. Mexican Relations and Chicano Culture*, ed. Renate von Bardeleben. Tubingen: Gunter Narrverlag, 1986.

Works Cited

"Código de las mujeres," *La Prensa*, San Antonio Texas, 16:4 (February 16, 1928), 7.

"Educad a la mujer," *El Regidor*, San Antonio, Texas, 8:332 (September 21, 1895), 3.

Gilbert, Sandra M. and Susan Gubar. *The Madwoman in the Attic.* New Haven: Yale University Press, 1979.

"La verdadera mujer," *La Prensa*, San Antonio, Texas, 16:41 (March 24, 1928), 7.

"Los mandamientos," *El Regidor*, San Antonio, Texas, 9:376 (August 27, 1896), 2.

"Lozano, un educador del Mexico de Afuera dice el señor Ortiz," *La Prensa*, San Antonio, Texas, 26:1 (February 13, 1938), Tercera Sección, 8.

"Más de cuatrocientos periódicos en español se han editado en los Estados Unidos," *La Prensa*, San Antonio, Texas, 26:1 (February 13, 1938), Tercera Sección, 7.

"Rasgos Biográficos De Pablo Cruz," *El Regidor*, San Antonio, Texas, 22:1072 (August 18, 1910), 1.

"Virtud," *El Regidor*, San Antonio, Texas, 9:372 (July 7, 1896), 2.

Yvonne Yarbro-Bejarano

Primer encuentro de lesbianas feministas latinoamericanas y caribeñas

The First Meeting of Latin American and Caribbean Feminist Lesbians took place October 14-17, 1987 in Cuernavaca, Mexico. Over 250 women from Central and South America, the U.S. and Canada, as well as Latin American women living in political or economic exile in England and Europe attended. During the three days of the conference, workshops were held on topics such as self-defense, lesbian mothers, healing and spirituality, sexuality, points of division and unity among Latin American lesbians, and the history and problems of lesbian organizations.

The formation of a Latin American and Caribbean lesbian network became the consuming topic of the conference by the afternoon of the third day, involving lengthy, and at times extremely heated discussions in which political, personal and cultural differences became painfully apparent. The contingent of approximately 30 Chicanas and Latinas living in the U.S. reacted strongly to an initial proposal excluding them from membership in the network. This exclusion was based on the perceived differences of living in the First World as opposed to the Third World. By the end of the conference, it was made overwhelmingly clear that this proposal represented a minority position, and the final decision did include Latinas living in the U.S. and other countries outside Latin America as full members in the network. However, the experience did remind us that many Latin American women do not have a full understanding of the racism and classism, the social, linguistic and cultural discrimination that define the reality of Latinas and Chicanas living in the U.S.

On the afternoon of the second day, a workshop was scheduled on lesbian identity, including sexuality. This will be the focus of my report, since the theme of the present issue of *Third Woman* is Latina sexuality. There was so much interest in this workshop that it was divided into four smaller groups to facilitate discussion. What struck me was that the women in my group approached the topics of roles and sexuality not so much in terms of sexual desire, but how they play themselves out in the contexts of personal relationships and lesbian organizations. It was not clear to me if this stemmed from a reluctance to talk about sex due to social and cultural conditioning or the understandable fear of revealing very private feelings to complete strangers.

One of the issues raised in the workshop was also addressed during the discussions of lesbian organizations: how sexual relationships between its members affect the life of an organization. While the possibility of forming sexual/emotional bonds with the lesbians we work with was seen as positive, as opposed to the lack of that option in mixed heterosexual or feminist heterosexual political groups, the prevailing concern was that scenarios surrounding sexual liaisons within the group often end up dividing or even destroying the organization: jealousy may arise if another person in the group has been attracted to one of the women involved; the new couple may be so involved with each other that they create an aura of exclusiveness around themselves that alienates the other members of the organization; if the couple breaks up, problems arise surrounding both of them staying in the group; if one of them gets involved with still another member of the organization after the break-up, more tension is generated; the couple may leave the group because they are so involved with each other that this focus replaces their interest in the organization, or perhaps it turns out that they joined the group to find a lover in the first place. This problem raises important issues of personal and collective responsibility. The women sexually involved have to weigh their personal desires against the good of the group as a whole, and the group must decide how to deal collectively with any conflicts that arise as a result of these internal relationships.

The greatest part of the discussion was dedicated to roles that represent the internalization of destructive heterosexual patterns. Many examples were given of lesbian couples that replicate the worst models of male-domination/female-subordination, in which one partner assumes a macho attitude vis-a-vis her partner, controlling her behavior, exhibiting jealousy and possessiveness, and upholding the sexual division of labor, while the other assumes the role of "wife," of passive sexual property. Some women said that when they first came out, they found themselves acting and dressing butch or femme, but that as they became more sure of their lesbian identity, they ceased to feel the need for these roles. The consensus seemed to be in the direction of escaping rigid labels or confinement to one or the other role. The desire for the freedom to incorporate both butch and femme within a single lesbian identity may be a response to the excessive prescriptiveness of role behavior within the Latina lesbian culture. On the other hand, since the butch/femme phenomenon is more prevalent among working-class Latinas, the critique expressed in the workshop may also be a factor of the predominantly middle-class identity of the women present.

One issue discussed in the workshop appears to be of equal concern to white lesbians in the U.S., if a glance through the recent literature is any indication: the waning of sexual desire in long-term lesbian relationships. Many women reported that their experience of relationships at the beginning are very exciting and intense sexually. As time goes by, sex becomes more and more infrequent, although the relationship may continue to be satisfying in other ways. The women who talked about this problem were concerned, not only with the loss of sexual expression, but also because in many cases the relationship ends when one or the other becomes sexually attracted to someone else, and the cycle begins again. Some women suggested that the problem was caused by excessive "merging" of the two individuals into one. One solution proposed was that the partners each attempt to remain more independent, more individually identified within the relationship, by cultivating separate interests and friends, and taking pains to have "time-out" away from her partner, whether alone or with friends. Some wondered if the problem had something to do with the lack of "difference" in the lesbian relationship, and that perhaps roles such as butch/femme in some ways help the couple to differentiate themselves.

Another major topic of discussion was the structure of lesbian relationships. This issue emerged from several women's concern with how to deal with the pain of breaking up. One response was to try to turn the pain into something creative, for example writing or painting, to some way get through the loss with the feeling that you have kept something of the relationship. Many women expressed dissatisfaction with the pattern of getting into a relationship, they think "for keeps," only to find themselves after six months, two years, or more, going through the pain of breaking up all over again. Some women thought the problem had to do with the desire to model lesbian relationships on heterosexual marriage, a model that may set up lesbians for this feeling of failure when it doesn't work out. It was suggested that perhaps the model of heterosexual marriage is not the best one for lesbians, and that we should explore alternatives, rather than imagine that this is the only way lesbians can be in relationships.

The question of alternatives to monogamous marriage, even if in reality the lesbian pattern may be one of "serial monogamy"—a succession of committed, monogamous relationships—brought up other questions. Some women wondered if the monogamous marriage might be a way of handling guilt about lesbian sexuality. For example, a lesbian might be sexually attracted to someone and act on it, but then finds herself building a relationship with a woman out of a reluctance to admit that what it was, was basically sex. People were equally unwilling to validate casual or promiscuous sex, but were interested in the possibility that internalized homophobia may result in the desire to legitimate lesbian desire in the closest thing to acceptable heterosexual relationships.

To sum up, the discussion of lesbian sexuality was marked by a sense of flexibility as opposed to rigid roles and structures, a desire to keep the fire alive in long-term unions and an openness to alternatives. The next meeting is tentatively set for 1989 in Peru, where some of these issues will no doubt be aired again.

Ana Castillo

The Distortion of Desire

Roosters, by Milcha Sánchez-Scott, in *American Theatre,* September 1987, pp 1-11.

The distortion of female sexuality within the confines of male-dominated Mexican/Latino culture has long been noted and discussed, we have the abundant resource of men's literature from which to illustrate this point. Only "man" as creator of all universal knowledge, may be viewed as the subject of desire, and in turn, designate the object of desire, as well as deny that status to whomever he chooses. To "woman", two classical roles have been assigned that may be traced to the roots of all myths throughout history—that of virgin/mother/nature on the one hand, whore/witch/mystic, on the other.

For this reason it is no wonder that from within such a structured cultural context where men alone may desire freely and therefore be desirable, an insightful woman who is coming of age would suffer not a small degree of psychological trauma. Such is the case with Angela, the adolescent daughter in *Roosters*. At her age, she does not only begin to develop into a specific gender type, but has begun to "feel" her emerging sexuality as well.

In *Roosters*, man as omnipotent being is a clearly stated idea. Religion, embedded culturally and socially into the psyche of the adolescent female, is seen as both the metaphor for her own desire and relentless faith in her father, and as the only escape from the fearful expectation of disappointment in the material world. Angela, praying fervently, looks to the sky and invokes a new trinity, "Holy Father, Abuelo, Hector, breathe life into me" (Act Two, Scene 4). In one line, Angela has called upon the patriarchs of her world—Holy Father (synonymous with her own father), her grandfather, and finally, Hector, her older brother and heir to the patriarchy. From these commanders and creators of her universe she asks to be given life.

In an early scene in Act One, Hector attempts to dissuade her from her fervent escape to a celestial fantasy by reminding her of her inevitable and most evident womanhood. "Stop hiding", he says. "You can't be a little girl forever." Angela, who has taken to dressing her dolls as saints, ignores him, and pretends to speak for the doll named St. Lucy: "They took my eyes because I wouldn't put out!" Hector responds by addressing the saint dolls: ". . . Miss Angela lies in her little, white, chaste, narrow bed, underneath the crucifix and masturbates!" He continues, despite Angela's obvious anger with him, "Just be yourself. A normal, sex-crazed, fifteen-year-old girl with a big gigantic enormous butt." He exits and again Angela resumes her prayer to heaven hoping to be spared of womanhood: "Send me a contraction/ A shriveling antidote/ make me little again/. . . Give me back my little butt."

The cause of such anxiety cannot be denied when one first encounters her two female role models in Scene 2, Act One. Aunt Chata, whom the playwright describes as "giv[ing] new meaning to the word blowsy", is sitting on the front porch steps, legs spread, fanning herself. Angela's mother, Juana, (virgin/mother/nature) self-described as "plain", rocks in a chair, hands folded on her lap. They are both waiting for the men, the return of the warriors, deemers and takers of woman's desire. In this scene, Juana is reflective and is coming upon the tragic realization that due to her plainness, her physical undesirability, (as defined by men/her husband/her son), she has become nothing more than a beast of burden. Angela, who is listening to the conversation between the two women, sisters-in-law and childhood friends, protests suddenly, "Mama, I don't wanna be plain."

Here, one is given the first clue that Angela has already decided and accepted her sexuality as it is defined within the confines of a macho-ruled family, she is presented with two options—to become the whore-aunt, who at 40 is viewed as pathetic and ridiculous or to follow her mother's long suffering role as one who waits. On the one hand, she may become a whore who acknowledges and acts upon her sexual desire but has nothing to expect from it but abandonment, and on the other, she waits for her desire to be acknowledged if only vicariously through a man. Most definitely, Angela does not want to be left waiting as her mother, and if she is going to be able to act upon her desire at all, she had better not be plain. Simultaneously, she understands to give vent to this desire means eternal damnation and so returns to her prayer for rescue.

Just as woman is taught by her religion and by her cultural

mores to negate sexual desire, man is taught to acknowledge his sexuality, which means to recognize desire in whatever form it takes in his surroundings. When Hector tells his young sister in Act One, Scene 3, that she has developed a "big, gigantic, enormous butt", in whatever manner an actor may choose to deliver these potent lines—and quite often, the playwright herself has chosen to deviate from the fuller development of such topics by interjecting lines that have no other purpose than comic relief—the suggestion of the trespassing of a taboo of brother/sister sexual relations cannot be ignored.

In Act Two, this suggestion takes full bloom at the end of Scene 4. Chata and her nephew Hector have a confrontation. Chata scolds Hector by reminding him that as long as his father is around there is no room for two *Roosters* in the yard. Hector, who is not *her* man, nor his mother's, must realize that the issue of who is *Rooster* is not tied to economic responsibility, (since Hector does more to support the family than the father) but to prowess, virility, the power of conquest. Hector, at last beaten down by Chata's argument, falls to his knees, (and this is where Angela's panicked religious devotion proves to have sound reason for existence), and asks his aunt, "Did you sleep with my father? Did he yearn for you as you slept in your *little, white, chaste, narrow bed?* Did he steal you when you were dreaming?" [italics mine] Chata, (not the young virginal Angela but the woman who long ago conceded to her sexuality) tells her nephew, "You're just like him, so handsome you make my teeth ache." Hector responds, "Whore, mother, sister, saint-woman, moon woman, give me the shelter of your darkness, fold me like a fan, and take me into your stillness, submerge me beneath the water, beneath the sea, beneath the mysteries, baptize me, bear me up, give me life, breathe on me." Is it man then that through his sexual desire returns to his primal contact with woman and knows in the deepest recesses of his mind that it is *he* who has been the one created and given life by woman, not the other way around? Although by experiencing her "mysteries" he will in some way claim his godlike state and take his rightful place to rule over her.

But this provocative theme is thwarted and ultimately diffused by the final scene when the play takes a conventional course. Hector takes his father's challenge and is able to overpower him in a knife fight. This delights the father in the knowledge that he has produced a cock no less a warrior than himself. Hector chooses to spare his father's life but it is clear who will be the rooster that will run the yard from then on. The father's once aggressive character is further diminished by a comical portrayal at the end of the play that renders him totally harmless as he soundlessly sleeps in complacent Juana's arms.

During this last scene, Angela has allowed herself to succumb to her desire for her biological father—for his protection, love, and acknowledgement. She appears in a caricaturesque costume of the desirable woman, her mother's old party dress, her aunt's cheap jewelry, and an overuse of makeup. She is waiting for her father to take her away with him as promised. When he doesn't, having permitted herself to be conned by him, she receives her first major disappointment as a woman who chooses to act on her desire.

At the end of the play, Angela, who has been praying arduously for redemption for having strayed from her only permitted devotion to man—a heavenly god—suddenly to the surprise of all begins to levitate. But even as she is being "restored" she calls from her levitated place in the air to the new family patriarch, the new symbol of desire, her brother Hector, "Abuelo, Queen of Heaven, All the Saints, it is true, I am back . . . I am restored. I am . . . Hector, take me with you." Hector responds, "Everywhere. . . ."

Another false promise as his father had promised all the women in his life? If Hector accepted his place as paternal leader, will he use his power to suppress or distort his sister's desire as was done by his father with his mother and aunt? There is no indication that this will not eventually happen. None of the characters in *Roosters* ever undergoes a convincing or complete transition from the limitations of their culturally defined role. There is no reason to anticipate that Angela, the woman, will be any less distorted in her sexual identity than the women and the men who surround her.

Cherríe Moraga

Algo secretamente amado

Borderlands/La frontera: The New Mestiza by Gloria Anzaldúa.
San Francisco: Spinsters/Aunt Lute, 1987. 203pp. $8.95

> *En este oscuro monte de nopal*
> *Algo secretamente amado*
> *Se oculta en mi vientre*
> *Y en mi corazón se incuba*
> *Un amor que no es de este mundo* (144).

Borderlands/La Frontera is a *mezcla* of writings—historical, philosophical, autobiographical, and poetic—which explores the creation of what Gloria Anzaldúa calls "the new mestiza". It addresses a vast number of feminist concerns within the sociohistorical context of the Chicano Southwest. The book is divided into two parts—the first, a series of essays; the second, a selection of poetry. Defying easy categorization, *La Frontera* is at its core the testimony *de una mujer que cree que su* "amor . . . no es de este mundo." The revelation of the fundamental alienation of the brown woman reflects a radical departure from traditional Chicano letters.

As a personal testimony, Anzaldúa not only tells her story, but attempts to derive philosophical meaning from her experience. Since her identity as a mestiza lesbian—mixed blood and female—refuses the rigid restrictions imposed by Western dualistic thinking, she challenges this basic tenet and suggests that a "mestiza consciousness" could eradicate the social ills it has created. She writes:

> The work of *mestiza* consciousness is to break down the subject-obect duality which keeps her a prisoner and to show in the flesh and through images in her work how duality is transcended. The answer to the problem between the white race and the colored, between males and females, lies in healing the split that originates in the very foundation of our lives, our culture, our languages and our

thoughts. A massive uprooting of dualistic thinking in the individual and collective consciousness is the beginning of a long struggle, but one that could, in our best hopes, bring us to the end of rape, of violence, of war. (80)

Ironically, *La Frontera* manifests the author's own inability to wholly reconcile this dualism. The writing is the strongest when she in fact does allow the *images* in her work to transcend the duality; the weakest, when the language objectifies and abstracts experience. One of the most moving images in the book is Anzaldúa's description of the border between the U.S. and México as a "1,950 mile-long open wound . . ."

> dividing a *pueblo*, a culture,
> running down the length of my body,
>   staking fence rods in my flesh,
>   splits me splits me
>   *me raja me raja* (2)

The image holds, speaks to something more profound than the intellectual knowledge of the loss of half our territory to the U.S. with the signing of the Treaty of Guadalupe in 1848. It speaks of a collective wound we remember as a people and proffers the possibility of healing. This vision informs the entire book.

However, where the author tries to analyze or attempts to describe that which seems to defy logic—such as Anzaldúa's metaphysical experiences—the writing becomes self-conscious and laborious. This is most evident in the chapter entitled "La herencia de Coatlicue," where the imagery seems to float, disconnected from its point of reference ("protean being/ dark dumb windowless," 41) and where the prose disorients, jumping around from anecdote to philosophy to history to *sueño*, seldom developing a single topic. Anzaldúa tells us she "was two or three years old the first time *Coatlicue* visited (her) psyche, the first time (she) . . . fell into the underworld" (42). And yet, she fails to provide a cogent understanding of her lived relationship to Coatlicue's visitations.

Anzaldúa is at heart a *cuentista*. In *La Frontera* "cuentos" (largely autobiographical) are interspersed throughout the essay. Through the cuento her most powerful imagery surfaces and once again that reconciliation she seeks as a mestiza writer is realized. Although she professes "that nothing happens in the 'real' world

Santa Barraza Coatlicue

unless it first happens in our heads," (a point with which Buddhists and Marxists alike would take issue), (87), her cuentos suggest the opposite. By re-living the "real" material experiences in writing, her "head" is able to interpret them for herself and the reader, and the collective wound is soothed!

> "It's been a bad year for corn," my brother, Nune says. As he talks, I remember my father scanning the sky for a rain that would end the drought, looking up into the sky, day after day, while the corn withered on its stalk. My father has been dead for 29 years, having worked himself to death. (90)

Similarly in some of the poetry—which is more narrative than lyrical—the mestiza/o reality takes on flesh. In "En el nombre de todas las madres que han perdido sus hijos en la guerra," (160) Anzaldúa gives voice to a Central American woman, mourning the murder of her child by soldiers: "Sentí que el niño apretó su manita/ la que tenía alrededor de mi dedo gordo/ Sangre saltó como agua aventada de una cubeta."

In "Yo no fui, fue Tete," the speaker, like the Central American mother, responds to the question of violence. Here a gay Chicano describes being assaulted on the street: "sentí la navaja/ esas miradas enloquecidas/ y tienen los huevos de llamarnos 'locas'/ que vergüenza, mi misma raza/ jijo 'ela chingada" (142). Through characters such as these, conventional dualities—male/female, heterosexual/homosexual—are dissolved and the subjects become one in their lament. Both poems give testimony to the author's stated identification with those who suffer racism, sexism, and homophobia—*todos (los) mexicanos on both sides of the border.*

Yet, Anzaldúa fails to speak to *todos (los) mexicanos* when the poems become "mini-essays," convoluted with "new age" and psychological jargon. In the poem, "Letting Go" for example, Anzaldúa describes the process of opening oneself up: "It's not enough/ deciding to be open" (164). But the poem is unclear as to what we must open ourselves—personal relationships, creative work? Image is built upon image, yet the actual material circumstances of the *lucha* are never mentioned. In this case, to which Mexicanos/as is Anzaldúa speaking—the Chicana lesbian like herself?

Ironically, the most profound message of *La Frontera* I believe has very little to do with lesbianism—lesbianism in the sexual sense. With the exception of the poem, "Compañera, cuando amábamos," there is very little physical description of lesbian sexuality. Lesbian desire is not a compelling force in the book. In fact, desire in the sexual sense is noticeably absent—whether heterosexual or lesbian. What *is* evident is the longing for the self—both physically and spiritually: "Algo secretamente amado/ . . . Un amor que no es de este mundo." Since the self is female, the love of self has been interpreted by many feminist thinkers as a "lesbian" quest, Adrienne Rich is a case in point. I concur with them that it is a quest upon which both lesbians and heterosexual women can enter, but maintain the definition of lesbianism as fundamentally about sexual desire between women. The love of self for the woman of color is not of this world because this racist and misogynist world does not allow it. Anzaldúa states, "I made the choice to be queer" (19). What I believe Anzaldúa is speaking to here is her *political* decision to identify herself as a lesbian. She adds parenthetically, "for some it is genetically inherent," (19) a comment I found particularly disturbing in that it throws us back to the 19th-century where medical "experts" attributed lesbianism to biological factors (See Richard von Krafft-Ebing's *Psychopathia Sexualis*). Her statement also suggests that those who believe their "genes made them do it" are the only ones who do not have a choice. The majority of women who have known that they were lesbians from a very early age do not feel they "chose" their sexuality, but attribute it to social factors and/or luck—certainly not to physiology or politics, for that matter. What makes the author "queer," however, is not her sexuality per se, but her desire to find and love herself amid the myriad lies and distortions told about her. It forces her from her home and further out into the margins, into that "border culture" between worlds. It is not a choice. She perceives it as a matter of survival:

> If going home is denied me then I will stand and claim my space, making a new culture—*una cultura mestiza*—with my own lumber, my own bricks and mortar and my own feminist architecture. (22)

That is precisely what *La Frontera* attempts to do. The pages become a kind of blueprint for *la nueva cultura* that Anzaldúa envisions. Oftentimes, the symbols are so coded only the architect can interpret them and only to herself. But the best of the writing wroughts out a vision from a suffering which Anzaldúa does not objectify, but lives. Like the *indocumentada*, Anzaldúa is a "refugee (who) leaves the familiar and safe homeground to venture into unknown and . . . dangerous terrain" (13). This is *La Frontera* and "this is her home this thin edge of barbwire" (13).

Cherríe Moraga

The Obedient Daughter

Trini, by Estela Portillo Trambley. Tempe, AZ: Bilingual Press/Editorial Bilingüe, 1986. 248pp. $8.95.

Trini by Estela Portillo Trambley was required reading for my Latina Literature course in 1986. Since I was teaching the course from a feminist perspective we examined texts on the basis of whether or not they reflected a woman-identified view of the Chicana/Latina experience; that is, one which seriously grapples with the lived reality of race/sex/class oppression and which, by definition, does something that male literature doesn't do. *Trini* does depict a brown woman confronting the very real hardships in the life of *una indocumentada* (such as rape, single motherhood, poverty, etc.), but the events of her life are shaped and understood through male-imposed definitions.

On the surface, the story is supposed to be about a Mexican woman with strong ties to her Tarahumara indigenous heritage, who illegally crosses the border to make a life for herself in the U.S. But looking more closely, one discovers that the immigrant woman is not really the subject of *Trini* at all, but the object. The portrayal of Trini does little more than once again objectify, through romanticization, the Mexican female and indigenous experience.

The opening scene (chronologically the book's end) describes Trini's encounter with a gringo artist, who is so taken by her that he wishes to paint her. She agrees. The result is a portrait which she believes captures her exactly, even amid "so many brown women faceless in the world....It is me," she states, being the most impressed by "the feet, bare, brown, seeming to grow out of the earth itself" (8). There is little about the description that does more than render the brown woman, once again, as earth/mother, the usual mystification that most males effect of the indigenous woman. That is not to say that reverence for earth may not be an authentic experience for the brown woman, but the author's description of the gringo's perception does little to move beyond stereotypes:

The figure of Trini on canvas was painted into the light, almost as if it had appeared out of the depth of rocks and earth. The whole body was a movement of strength, sustained, yet free. There was something mystical about her eyes, dark, looking to the level of the living, yet seeing beyond. The hair flew loose and long with the wind. (8)

There is no critique or criticism of such objectification. Instead it becomes increasingly evident that the author herself subscribes to the same romantic view of the brown woman.

Thematically, the book explores a variety of subjects of concern to Chicana literature: the Latina as *extranjera* in the U.S., the bicultural experience, traditional catholicism vs. the spirituality of *indigenismo*, and the conflict of our *mestizaje*. Early on, we observe Trini pulled by both sides of herself—the white and the indian. At times, she experiences herself as the fertility goddess, Tonantzin, and is much more drawn to the brown clay image, than to the "pretty painted little Virgin" (73). And yet, Trini believes that her devotion to the Catholic Virgin helped her make the crossing to the U.S. Although she ultimately makes a comfortable life for herself in the U.S., her primal longings are associated with the pre-Christian/pre-Columbian world of the indigenous—longings which when experienced, she always describes as "the green blood surging." (The image is repeated often in the novel, but in its obvious literal association with the color of nature, it provided little depth to Trini's character.)

Her desire to reclaim and affirm her true spirit (that indigenous spirit the gringo artist exactly captured) is the major conflict for Trini; and, as in the tradition of all women's romances (Harlequin, etc.), the means and the end to her conflict is a man. Through Sabochi, the Tarahumara Indian who first serves as Trini's surrogate "mother"/protector after the death of her mother, and then later as her lover, the protagonist yearns for the fulfillment of a longing she cannot name. The longing is clearly sexual in that through Sabochi, Trini first discovers her womanhood, consummates her longing in the sex act, and ultimately finds meaning in her life through his offspring. Here Portillo first describes the adolescent Trini's feelings:

> She did not follow the children. There was a ringing of the senses that touched every fiber of her body. She threw her

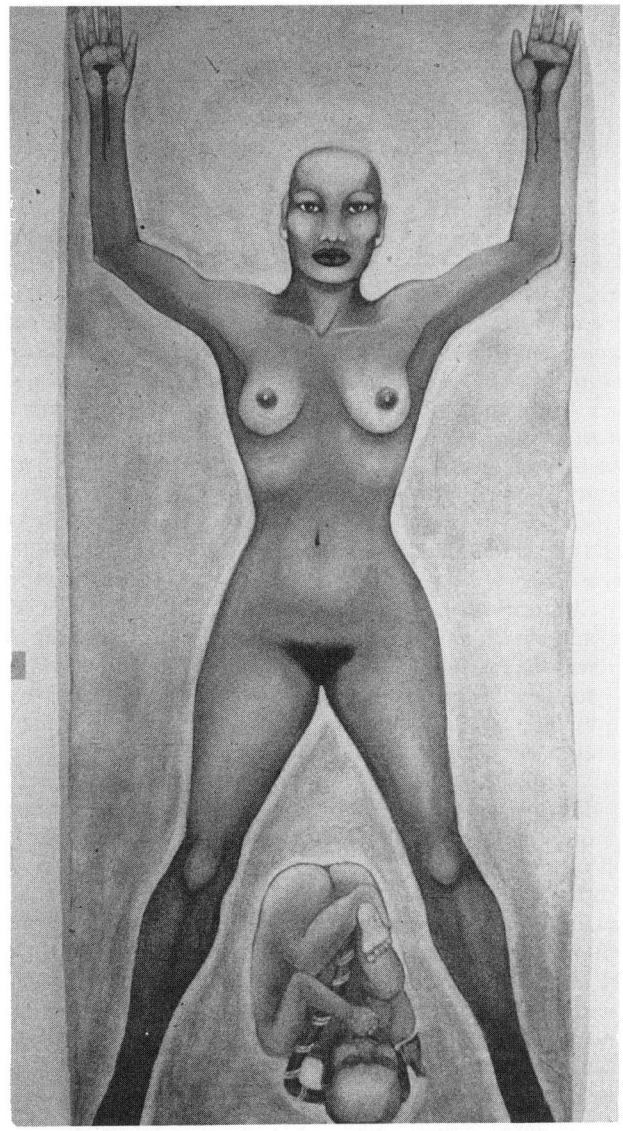

Cecilia Alvarez   Los eternos sacrificios

arms around his chest, feeling the beat of his heart, . . . She looked up at his face, wishing to find something . . . She wanted to shout at him, "I'm a woman! A woman! Take me with you." She ached with the wanting. But there were no words. She touched his face, thirsting not to forget—line of jaw, the gentle mouth, the eyes so full of the universe. (22)

From these earliest passages, the story proceeds with Sabochi presented as the "noble savage." The author romanticizes him to be the answer to this unrequited desire from which Trini suffers throughout the novel. Like all good "romances," the love object escapes the protagonist's grasp throughout most of the story. Trini is separated from Sabochi through marriage to Tonio, a *mujeriego* who represents the fate of most women of having to settle for less than their dreams in an unhappy marriage. Interestingly, Portillo's depiction of the "real" fate of most Mexican women is much more tangible and compelling than the superficial romances to which the novel subscribes:

That night Tonio lays beside her, big and blunt, protected in a dreary silence, the dark wrapped around him, his back stubbornly to her. He was denying her. Shame suffocated her, but she would be as ungiving as he. How many times had she reached out for him, forgiving? She knew that he was not awake because he did not care. She felt inept for wanting him and not having him, for having lost that freedom of forgiving. (244)

That sense of estrangement from a partner is one so common to our experience and Portillo describes it with the sensitivity of one who knows. Other elements of the female experience are also realistically presented. After Trini is raped, her Tía Pancha prepares a hot bath for her in a kind of healing ritual, grounded in recognition of rape as a reality all women must live with. Trini asks, "What's to become of me now?" and Tía Pancha responds, "You go on with your life" (104). Of course. But when Sabochi enters the scene to avenge the rape by murdering the rapist, we know the novel has once again fallen into the trap of romantic illusion, where our male hero is described, not as cowboy on a white horse, but a "Tarahumara, who moved like lighting" (122). The myth of male protection from male violence is just that—a myth—for most women of color are not given protection in the Male State. When Trini's longings for the Tarahumara is finally consummated, she experiences a kind of metaphysical union with the earth. In love-making, her red blood turns into the green color of nature. Although, *she* is woman, *he* is her connection to the earth. Even powers she has associated with the female Tonantzin are not accessible to Trini, except through man as medium:

> Green blood glistened, throbbed, ran through arteries, cutting the moon, shifting the light, until the earth exploded, gaping wide for green waters, green blood, soft, soft. The earth was all inside her. All was body, beyond body, for body. (170)

But, of course, this is a love not to be possessed, according to the natural law of Sabochi, the free spirit. "She had seen it before when she was a little girl, when the urge to roam grew strong in him. She understood the hunger, the hunger to return to what he was, to what he would always be..." (171). And yet, she does possess something of the man, his seed. The boy/child he was given her, Rico "whose eyes spoke a bond of feeling that Trini knew could only have come from those ancient mountains in her past" (242). In contrast, the female child, Linda (from Tonio's seed), is described as someone insensitive to the fragility of nature. Through Rico, Trini once again experiences her connection with Sabochi and the sensation of "the green blood surging" (244). Portillo states, "The earth was all still inside her, waiting. She must go to Sabochi again, soon..." (244). In revealing to Rico who his real father is—"a noble man, a man of freedom" (245)—Trini is vindicated of a marriage that has failed her.

Her purpose as female has been fulfilled in that her offspring, as indigenous male, would realize the destiny of the Tarahumaras, a realization that Trini, as female, feels she is unable to attain herself. Portillo tells us, "she knew that Rico would let the seed grow inside him" (244). She, as woman, is the vessel of the continuation of the patrilineal legacy.

The fundamental male-centered resolution in *Trini* brings to mind another work by the author, *The Day of the Swallows*, a play published in 1969. I've always loved *Swallows*, although it is a "classic" lesbian work in the worse sense of a 1950's view where all lesbian protagonists are punished for their disobedience to the male hegemony. They all end up dead or howling at the moon on all fours in a crazed frenzy, as does Josefa whose suicide is described as a sensuous reunion with the body of the lake. In this play, as in *Trini*, Portillo as author is the obedient daughter.* Those who follow the law of the father will be rewarded (thus, the "happy" ending in *Trini*); those who transgress are punished (the lesbian suicide). Still the value of *Swallows* remains in its daring and complex depiction of a lesbian who is actively desirous, whose desire is equal to the urges of a man, but who rightly fears for her life to face it.

But possibly I was too hungry in the 70's for a Chicana lesbian literature yet to be born; or possibly I *was* seeing something that was really there, but something which since then Portillo has been unwilling to explore further—the taboo subject of Mexican female desire. *Trini* sends us whirling backwards where the Mexican woman's suffering and sexuality is only justified through the male fruit of her labor. In short, *Trini* romanticizes heterosexuality with the indigenous serving as no more than a motif, adding *sabor* to the story. The novel does little for its Chicana readership, rendering us once again passive instruments in the male heroic quest. As such, Portillo has secured her position as obedient daughter to the Chicano patriarchal literary canon.

---

* Norma Alarcón explores this theme of "obedience/disobedience" in relation to Chicana literature in her essay, "Chicana's Feminist Literature: A Re-vision Through Malintzin/or Malintzin: Putting Flesh Back on the Object," in *This Bridge Called My Back: Writings by Radical Women of Color*, Gloria Anzaldúa and Cherríe Moraga, eds. New York: Kitchen Table: Women of Color Press, 1983, 182-190.

Alvina E. Quintana
La lucha continúa

The Mixquiahuala Letters by Ana Castillo. Tempe, AZ: Bilingual Press/Editorial Bilingüe, 1986. 132pp. $8.95.

Ana Castillo is by no means a new name to the Chicana literary circuit. Although she is a poet who has been widely anthologized, it was probably her first book-length collection of poetry, *Women Are Not Roses* (Arte Público Press, 1984), that brought her the most recognition. Positioning her as one of the primal voices in what we might refer to as "Chicana poetic feminism," *Roses* effectively set the agenda as it opened the dialogue and created a need to further explore themes of poetics, politics, and sexuality. With Castillo's latest work, the dialogue continues.

Mediating and challenging, *The Mixquiahuala Letters* resonates with the political forces of the 80's. The 80's reflect a time when dominant ideas and assumptions are constantly problematized because of their ideological implications—a moment when Chicanas, like other women of color, are coming to the front, philosophizing about a new kind of feminism.

Because the feminist theory that was inspired by the social upheaval of the 60's helped to perpetuate white middle-class values, it merely created new tensions for women of color in the United States. Proliferating from the printed word, these were tensions that grew stronger as they went unchallenged. Castillo's novel functions as an oppositional feminist discourse that challenges the inherent limitations brought about by both Anglo-American and Mexican culture. This is a novel of protest, actively questioning the "so-called" control of the patriarchy, striking out against the limitations placed on women.

In *The Mixquiahuala Letters* Castillo attempts to retaliate against social injustice and inequality by documenting what is at risk when the Chicana defies authority in order to break away from the stagnant traditions and ideals that smother and suppress female desire. Her poetic style adds new depth and beauty to women's literature. She explores the female psyche—the unspeakable, unveiling secrets and taboos in language that is profound and whimsical, perverse and waggish:

> In the musk halls
> of a sacrificial temple at the ruins of Monte Albán
> you changed your tampon
> before the eyes of gods, ghosts, and scorpions
> while i watched for mortals. (17)

Castillo's novel illustrates how Chicanas, caught between two cultures, move closer to self-discovery, by drawing and synthesizing usable aspects from both Anglo and Mexican cultures, weaving a complicated present from the traditional Mexican past and the Anglo-American future. The novel centers on the experiences of two friends, Teresa and Alicia, as they live, love and travel through México and the United States. Castillo uses the epistolary form as a vehicle, which enables her to move freely from one issue to another, from one country to another as she insightfully describes the relationship between the sexes:

> México. Melancholy, profoundly right and wrong, it embraces as it strangulates.
> Destiny is not a metaphysical confrontation with one's self, rather, society has knit its pattern so tight that a confrontation with it is inevitable.
> When we returned to México together we met our destiny at every stopover, pueblo, city café, on any bus, street, at the coast, peninsula, and central plateau. (59)

But more importantly, it is the epistolary form that gives her the flexibility to describe the differences between the way women are viewed in the United States and México. In an entry devoted to recollections about her experiences in Veracruz, Teresa recalls a conversation she had with Ponce, a Mexican engineer:

> He began, "I think you are a 'liberal woman.' Am I correct?" His expression meant to persuade me that it didn't matter what I replied. In the end he would win. He would systematically strip away all my pretexts, reservations and defenses, and end up in bed with me. In that country, the term

"liberated woman" meant something other than what we had strived for back in the United States. In this case; it simply meant a woman who would sleep nondiscriminately with any man who came along. I enhaled deeply from the strong cigarette he had given me and released the smoke in the direction of his face which diminished the sarcastic expression. (73).

It is with this sense of irony and humor that Castillo proceeds throughout her work.

In true post-modernist fashion, Castillo provides her readers with a pastiche of what has been a nearly invisible section of Chicano culture. Her fragmented approach becomes a powerful tool that enables her to negotiate and mediate, as she probes the Chicana experience. He prose reflects the influence and power of many of Latin America's greatest writers. And because of this, it comes as no surprise that she dedicates her novel to "the master of the game, Julio Cortázar".

With *The Mixquiahuala Letters*, Ana Castillo has moved beyond her role as Chicana poet onto the role of Chicana novelist and feminist critic, moving all Chicanas one step further on the path to self-discovery so that each one of us can, in Teresa's words, understand that "I was a woman, but I was first human."

Lourdes Torres

Risking All for Margarita

The Margarita Poems by Luz María Umpierre. Berkeley, CA: Third Woman Press, 1987. 48pp. $5.95.

Luz María Umpierre-Herrera has published four poetry collections to date: *Una puertorriqueña en Penna* (1979), *En el país de las maravillas* (1982), *Y otras desgracias/ and other misfortunes* (1985), and now *The Margarita Poems* (1987).

Like her other works, *The Margarita Poems* is filled with keen insights and biting commentary on the social and political scene with a special emphasis on the struggles of Latinas and Latinos in the United States and abroad. As an island born Puerto Rican woman who now lives and works in the United States, Umpierre's perspective bridges both worlds. Her creative manipulation of English, Spanish, and code-mixing render her poetry linguistically intriguing.

The latest collection is indeed revolutionary. Umpierre has always challenged conventional notions about gender roles and sexuality; however, in *The Margarita Poems*, the poet "Comes Out" in totally explicit, painfully direct, and lyrically erotic language.

While the collection works on many levels, for me, it works most powerfully as an encounter with obsessive love with all its passion, exhilaration, and agony. The nine poems of this exciting volume lead us into the body and soul of a possessed lover. In "Immanence", the first poem, the speaker calls forth Julia, the muse, the wild woman in the speaker who will lead her to Margarita, the object of desire. Julia is summoned to release the speaker and give her the strength to explore her lesbian self, regardless of the serious risks involved.

As the collection progresses it appears that the release of the wild woman has negative repercussions. The speaker has risked all for Margarita. Her physical and especially her mental health have been jeopardized for the love of this woman which is unrequited.

Margarita's rejection, however, is not the only obstacle the speaker must confront. In some of the poems the struggle is between the woman who demands the right to her sexual identity and those forces in a heterosexist society which seek to repress homosexual love. In "No Hatchet Job", for example, many agents conspire to bring down the poet. The insecure people around her sadistically dream of bringing her down to their shallow depths, but the woman/poet stubbornly survives. She will continue to write, to love whom she chooses despite the malicious attempts to silence her.

Breaking yet another taboo Umpierre links lesbianism to a woman's love for her mother. "Madre" is a beautifully erotic tribute to the mother. The speaker in this poem declares that she seeks closeness and understanding of her mother through the erotic love of lesbian women. The poem is shocking in that the love of the mother is placed on the same level as sexual, lesbian love. In fact, lesbian love is presented as a means of knowing the mother. The speaker, upon consummating her love with the chosen Margarita proclaims,

Y heme aquí hoy, madre,
intoxicada en jugos de Margarita
feliz, al fin de conocerte
y saborearte en este líquido rojo
que escapa por mi piel.

"Ceremonia Secreta" works as an introduction to the final work of the collection. The speaker, now deserted by her sometimes lover Margarita, is alone, heartbroken and almost defeated. She searches obsessively for the elusive lover. While friends try to help, no substitute will do. In desperation she seeks the aid of supernatural forces which promise to help conjure Margarita forward. Margarita is presented as a prisoner of her own making; the task at hand is to liberate her from herself.

"The Mar/Garita Poem" is the culmination of the search. The search developed throughout the collection progresses as more than a search for the woman/idol. The search emerges also as a yearning for liberty, liberty for lesbians, for Latinas, and for the Caribbean. A new language must be created in order to free Mar/Garita. From the depths of despair and oppression the speaker realizes that she is alone. She can no longer rely on others. The poet must invent a new language that will speak her truths, a language that will liberate Margarita from herself, and free the speaker from the other forces that oppress her. She can only realize this liberation through the assistance of other women's voices. Solely through the transformation of other women's voices will the speaker be able to weave her own new language. With this help, the poet begins to shed her isolation. At this point the island which represents the speaker is symbolically united with Margarita.

The Margarita Poems represents a new dimension in the history of Puerto Rican poetry. The three introductions to the work, included in the text, praise the collection for both its stylistic and poetic achievements. But I think it also deserves to be celebrated as the first openly lesbian collection of love poems by a Puerto Rican woman.

Norma Alarcón

Chicana Writers and Critics in a Social Context: Towards a Contemporary Bibliography*

I. Poetry

Abrego, Carmen. *Women In My Lost Dreams.* n.p., 1985.
Acosta, Teresa Palomo. *Passing Time.* n.p., 1984.
Aguilar-Henson, Marcela. *figura cristalina.* Edited by Norma Cantú. San Antonio, TX: M&A Editions, 1983.
Anzaldúa, Gloria. *Borderlands, La Frontera.* San Francisco: Spinsters/Aunt Lute, 1987.
Bornstein-Somoza, Miriam. *Bajo Cubierta.* 2nd edition. Tucson, AZ: Scorpion Press, 1977.
Brinson-Pineda, Barbara. See: Curiel, Barbara Brinson.
Candelaria, Cordelia. *Ojo de la Cueva.* Colorado Springs, Colorado: Maize Press, 1984.
Castellano, Olivia. *Blue Mandolin, Yellow Field.* Berkeley: Grito del Sol, quarterly books, year five, book three, 1980.
_____. *Blue Horse of Madness.* Sacramento, CA: Crystal Clear, 1983.
_____. *Spaces That Time Missed.* Sacramento, CA: Crystal Clear, 1986.
Castillo, Ana. *Otro Canto.* Chicago: Alternativa Publications, 1977.
_____. *The Invitation.* n.p., 1979. 2nd edition, 1986. (Available through *Third Woman.*)
_____. *Women Are Not Roses.* Houston: Arte Público Press, 1984.

---

*A few older texts are included in an effort to begin the arduous task of a more far-reaching bibliography. *Third Woman* would appreciate readers' help in this effort.

———. *My Father Was a Toltec.* Novato, CA: West End Press, 1988.
Catacalos, Rosemary. *Again For The First Time.* Santa Fe, New Mexico: Tooth of Time Books, 1984.
Cervantes, Lorna Dee. *Emplumada.* Pittsburgh, PA: University of Pittsburgh Press, 1981.
Cisneros, Sandra. *Bad Boys.* San Jose, CA: Mango Publications, 1980.
———. *My Wicked Wicked Ways.* Bloomington, IN: Third Woman Press, 1987.
Corpi, Lucha. *Palabras de Mediodía/Noon Words.* Translation by Catherine Rodríguez-Nieto. Berkeley, CA: El Fuego de Aztlán Publications, 1980.
Cota-Cárdenas, Margarita. *Noches despertando inconciencias.* Tucson, Arizona: Scorpion Press, 1977.
Curiel, Barbara Brinson. (Née Brinson-Pineda) *Nocturno.* Berkeley: El Fuego de Aztlán, 1978.
———. *Speak To Me From Dreams.* Berkeley, CA: Third Woman Press, 1989.
de Hoyos, Angelina. *Arise, Chicano and Other Poems.* Bilingual edition, traducciones de Mireya Robles. Bloomington, IN: Backstage Books, 1975.
———. *Selecciones.* Traducción del inglés por Mireya Robles. Veracruz, México: Taller Editorial, S.A., 1976.
———. *Chicano Poems: For the Barrio.* Aztlán: M&A Editions, 1977.
———. *Selected Poems/selecciones.* Spanish trans. by Mireya Robles. San Antonio, TX: Dezkalzo Press, 1979.
———. *Arise Chicano! and Other Poems.* Bilingual edition. Spanish translation by Mireya Robles. Revised and enlarged edition. San Antonio, Tejas: M&A Editions, 1980.
———. *Woman, Woman.* Houston, TX: Arte Público Press, 1985.
González, Beatriz. *The Chosen Few.* San Antonio, TX: M&A Editions, 1983.
Gonzáles, Rebecca. *Slow Work to the Rhythm of Cicadas.* Fort Worth, TX: Prickly Pear Press, 1985.
Gonzáles, Sylvia Alicia. *La Chicana Piensa, The Social-Cultural Conscious of a Mexican American Woman.* n.p., 1974.
Hernández Tovar, Inés. *Con Razón Corazón.* San Antonio: Caracol, 1977.

———. *Con Razón Corazón.* 2nd edition, enlarged. San Antonio, TX: M&A Editions, 1987.
Luera, Yolanda. *Solitaria J.* La Jolla, CA: Lalo Press Publications, 1986.
Martínez, Lorri. *Where Eagles Fall.* Brunswick, Maine: Blackberry, 1982.
Martínez, Marie. *Sterling Silver Roses.* San Francisco: La Morenita, 1981.
Mora, Pat. *Chants.* Houston: Arte Público Press, 1984.
———. *Borders.* Houston: Arte Público Press, 1986.
Moraga, Cherríe. *Loving in The War Years.* Boston: South End Press, 1983.
Moreno, Dorinda. *La mujer es la tierra/La tierra da vida.* Berkeley, CA: Casa Editorial, 1975.
Quiñonez, Naomi. *Sueño de Colibrí/Hummingbird Dream.* Los Angeles: West End Press, 1985.
Rivera, Marina. *Sobra.* San Francisco: Casa Editorial, 1977.
———. *Mestiza.* Tucson, Arizona: Grilled Flowers Special Issue Series, Number Two, 1977.
Rocha, Rina G. *Eluder.* Chicago: Alexander Books, 1980.
Romero, Lin. *Happy Songs, Bleeding Hearts.* San Diego: Toltecas en Aztlán Publications, 1974.
Sánchez, Pilar. *Symbols.* San Francisco: Casa Editorial Publications, 1975.
Schmidt, Lorenza Calvillo. *Poems.* In *First Chicano Literary Prize 1974-75.* Dept. of Spanish and Portuguese, Irvine: University of California, 1975.
Serrano, Nina. *Heart Songs, The Collected Poems of Nina Serrano (1969-1979).* San Francisco: Editorial Pocho-Che, 1980.
Silva, Beverly. *The Second St. Poems.* Ypsilanti, Mich.: Bilingual Press, 1983.
Tafolla, Carmen. *Get Your Tortillas Together.* San Antonio, TX: M&A Publications, 1976.
———. *Curandera.* San Antonio, TX: M&A Editions, 1983.
———. *Patchwork/Colcha.* Flagstaff, AZ: CEE Publications, 1987.
Trujillo-Gaitán, Marcela. *Chicano Themes: Manita Poetry.* Minneapolis: Chicano Studies, University of Minnesota, 1975.
Valdés, Gina. *Puentes y Fronteras.* Los Angeles: n.p., 1982.
———. *Comiendo Lumbre, Eating Fire.* Colorado Springs, CO: Maize Press, 1986.

Vigil, Evangelina. *nade y nade*. San Antonio, TX: M&A Editions, 1978.
_____. *Thirty an' Seen a Lot*. Houston: Arte Público Press, 1982.
Vigil-Piñon, Evangelina. *The Computer is Down*. Houston: Arte Público Press, 1987.
Villanueva, Alma. *Bloodroot*. Austin, TX: Place of Herons Press, 1977.
_____. *Mother, May I?* n.p.: Motheroot Publications, 1978.
_____. *Life Span*. Austin, TX: Place of Herons Press, 1985.
_____. "La Chingada". In *Five Poets of Aztlán*, Santiago Daydi-Tolson, ed., Tempe, AZ: Bilingual Review, 1985.
Xelina. *Ku*. San Antonio: Caracol, 1977.
Zamora, Bernice. *Restless Serpents*. Menlo Park, CA: Diseños Literarios, 1976.

II. Fiction

Castillo, Ana. *The Mixquiahuala Letters*. Binghamton, NY: Bilingual Press/Editorial Bilingüe, 1986.
_____. *Sapogonia*. Tempe, AZ: Bilingual Press/Editorial Bilingüe, 1989.
Chávez, Denise. *The Last of the Menu Girls*. Houston: Arte Público Press, 1986. Reprint 1987.
Cisneros, Sandra. *The House On Mango Street*. Houston: Arte Público Press, 1985.
_____. *The House on Mango Street*. 2nd, revised edition. Houston: Arte Público Press, 1988.
Corpi, Lucha. *Delia's Song*. Houston: Arte Público Press, 1989.
Cota-Cárdenas, Margarita. *Puppet*. Austin, TX: Relámpago Books, 1985.
del Fuego, Laura. *Maravilla*. Los Angeles: Floricanto Press, 1989.
Ornelas, Berta. *Come Down From the Mound*. Phoenix, Arizona: Miter Publishing Co., 1975.
Pineda, Cecile. *Face*. New York: Penguin Books, 1986.
_____. *Frieze*. New York: Penguin Books, 1987.
Ponce, Mary Helen. *Recuerdo: Short Stories of the Barrio*. Tujunga, CA: Adams & Associates, 1983.
_____. *Taking Control*. Houston: Arte Público Press, 1987.
Ranck, Katherine Quintana. *Portrait of Doña Elena*. Berkeley: Tonatiuh-Quinto Sol International, 1982.

Ríos, Isabella. *Victuum.* Ventura, CA: Diana-Etna Incorporated, 1976.
Ruíz de Burton, Marie Amparo. *The Squatter and the Don.* San Francisco: n.p., 1885.
Silva, Beverly. *The Cat and Other Stories.* Tempe, Arizona: Bilingual Press/Editorial Bilingüe, 1986.
Taylor, Shelia Ortiz. *Faultline.* Tallahassee, Fla.: Naiad Press, 1982.
_____. *Spring Forward/Fall Back.* Tallahassee, Fla.: Naiad Press, 1985.
Trambley, Estela Portillo. *Rain of Scorpions and Other Writings.* Berkeley: Tonatiuh International, 1975.
_____. *Trini.* Binghamton, NY: Bilingual Press/Editorial Bilingüe, 1986.
Valdés, Gina. *There Are No Madmen Here.* San Diego, CA: Maize Press, 1981.
Villanueva, Alma. *The Ultraviolet Sky.* Tempe, AZ: Bilingual Press/Editorial Bilingüe, 1988.
Viramontes, Helena Maria. *The Moths and Other Stories.* Houston: Arte Público Press, 1985.

III. Theater

Domínguez, Sylvia Maida. *La Comadre María.* Austin, TX: American Universal Artforms Corp., 1973.
Moraga, Cherríe. *Giving Up the Ghost.* Los Angeles: West End Press, 1986.
Trambley, Estela Portillo. "The Day of the Swallows." In *Contemporary Chicano Theatre,* Roberto J. Garza, ed. South Bend, IN: University of Notre Dame Press, 1976.
_____. *Sor Juana and Other Plays.* Ypsilanti, Mich.: Bilingual Press/Editorial Bilingüe, 1983.

IV. Autobiography, Autobiographical Essays, Biography and Oral Biohistory

Anzaldúa, Gloria. *Borderlands, La Frontera.* San Francisco: Spinsters/Aunt Lute, 1987.
Buss, Fran Leeper. *La Partera, Story of a Midwife.* Ann Arbor: University of Michigan Press, 1980.

Cabeza de Baca, Fabiola. *We Fed Them Cactus*. Albuquerque: University of New Mexico Press, 1979. First published 1954.

de la Guerra, María de las Angustias. *Occurrences in California*. Trans. Francis Price and William Ellison. Washington: Academy of American Franciscan History, 1956.

Elsasser, Nan, Kyle MacKenzie and Yvonne Tixier y Vigil. *Las Mujeres, Conversations from a Hispanic Community*. Old Westbury, NY: The Feminist Press; New York: McGraw-Hill Book Company, 1980.

Gamio, Manuel. *The Life Story of the Mexican Immigrant*. Chicago: University of Chicago Press, 1931. Reprinted, New York: Dover Publications, 1971.

García, Céline Frémaux. *Céline: Remembering Louisiana, 1850-1871*. Athens, GA: The University of Georgia Press, 1988.

Holden, William Curry. *Teresita* (Life of Teresa Urrea). Owings Mills, MD: Stemmer House, 1978.

Jaramillo, Cleofas. *Cuentos del hogar*. n.p., 1939.

_____. *Shadows of the Past*. n.p., 1941.

_____. *Romance of a Little Village*. San Antonio, TX: Naylor, 1955.

Moreno, Dorinda, ed. *La mujer en pie de lucha*. México: Espina del Norte publications, 1973.

Newby, Elizabeth Loza. *A Migrant with Hope*. Nashville: Groadman Press, 1977.

Niggli, Josefina. *Mexican Village*. Chapel Hill, NC: University of North Carolina Press, 1945.

_____. *Step Down Elder Brother*. New York: Rinehart, 1947.

Moraga, Cherríe. *Loving in the War Years*. Boston: South End Press, 1983.

Rodríguez, Gregorita. *Singing For My Echo*. As told to Edith Powers. Santa Fe, New Mexico: Cota Editions, Ocean Tree Services, 1987.

Warren, Nina Otero. *Old Spain in Our Southwest*. New York: Harcourt Brace and Co., 1936.

V. Anthologies: Poetry, Fiction, Essays

Agosin, Marjorie and Patricia Montenegro, eds. *Midwest-East,*

Midwest-West. Bloomington, IN: A Chicano-Riqueño Studies Publication, 1980.
Alvarado de Ricord, Elsie, Lucha Corpi and Concha Michel. *Fireflight.* Trans. by Catherine Rodríguez-Nieto. n.p. Oyez, 1976.
Boza, María del Carmen, Beverly Silva and Carmen Valle, eds. *Nosotras, Latina Literature Today.* Binghamton, NY: Bilingual Review/Press, 1986.
Gómez, Alma, Cherríe Moraga and Mariana Romo-Carmona, eds. *Cuentos: Stories by Latinas.* New York: Kitchen Table/Women of Color Press, 1983.
Sánchez, Rosaura, ed. *Requisa Treinta y Dos, Colección de Cuentos, Short Story Collection, Bilingual Edition.* La Jolla, CA: Chicano Research Publications, 1979.

VI. Critical Essays/Books on the Literature of Chicanas

Herrera-Sobek, María, ed. *Beyond Stereotypes, The Critical Analysis of Chicana Literature.* Binghamton, NY: Bilingual Press/Editorial Bilingüe, 1985.
Horno-Delgado, Asunción, Eliana Ortega, Nina M. Scott, and Nancy Saporta Sternbach. *Breaking Boundaries: Latina Writing and Critical Readings.* Amherst: University of Massachusetts Press, 1989.
Ramos, Luis Arturo. *Angela de Hoyos, A Critical Look.* Albuquerque: Pajarito Publications, 1979.
Sánchez, Marta Ester. *Contemporary Chicana Poetry.* Berkeley: University of California Press, 1985.
Yarbro-Bejarano, Yvonne. "The Female Subject in Chicano Theatre: Sexuality, 'Race' and Class." *Theatre Journal,* (December 1986), 389-407.

VII. Special Issues on the Literature of Chicanas/Latinas

Herrera-Sobek, María and Helena María Viramontes, eds. "Chicana Creativity and Criticism: Charting New

Frontiers in American Literature." Special issue *The Americas Review.* 15, 3-4 (1987).

Vigil, Evangelina, ed. "Woman of Her Word: Hispanic Women Write." Special issue *Revista Chicano-Riqueña.* XI:3-4 (1983).

El Grito. Year VII, book 1 (1973).

La Palabra. 2:2 (1980).

Revista Chicano-Riqueña. VI:2 (1978).

VIII. Chicana/Latina Feminist Theory

Alarcón, Norma. "What Kind of Lover Have You Made Me Mother?" In *Women of Color; Perspectives on Feminism and Identity,* Audrey T. McCluskey, ed. Occasional Papers Series, Vol. 1, No. 1. Bloomington, IN: Women's Studies Program, Indiana University, 1985.

_____. "Traddutora, Traditora: A Paradigmatic Figure of Chicana Feminism." In *Changing our Power: An Introduction to Women Studies,* Jo Whitehorse Cochran, Donna Langston, Carolyn Woodward, eds. Dubuque, Iowa: Kendall/Hunt Publishing Co., 1988.

Anzaldúa, Gloria and Cherríe Moraga, eds. *This Bridge Called My Back: Writings by Radical Women of Color.* Boston: Persephone Press, 1981. Second edition, New York: Kitchen Table Press, 1983.

Cotera, Martha P. *The Chicana Feminist.* Austin, TX: Information Systems Development, 1977.

Enríquez, Evangelina and Alfredo Mirandé. "Chicana Feminism." In their *La Chicana: The Mexican-American Woman.* Chicago: University of Chicago Press, 1979. 202-244.

Sánchez, Rita. "Chicana Writer Breaking Out of Silence." *De Colores* 3:3 (1977).

Tafolla, Carmen. *To Split A Human: Mitos, Machos y la Mujer Chicana.* San Antonio, TX: Mexican American Cultural Center, 1985.

Trujillo-Gaitán, Marcela. "The Dilemma of the Modern Chicana Artist and Critic." *De Colores* 3:3 (1977), 38-48. Reprinted in *Heresies* 8 (1979), 5-10 and in *The Third Woman,* Dexter Fisher, ed. Boston: Houghton Mifflin, 1980. 324-332.

IX. Chicana/Latina Journals

Comadre. 1977-? (Ceased)
Encuentro Femenil. 1973-? (Ceased)
Hijas de Cuauhtemoc. 1971-? (Ceased)
Intercambios Femeniles. 1984-Present.
Revista Mujeres. 1984-Present.
Third Woman. 1981-Present.

X. Books that include Critical Literature on Chicanas

Candelaria, Cordelia. *Chicano Poetry, A Critical Introduction.*
   Westport, CT, London, England: Greenwood Press, 1986.
Córdova, Teresa, Norma Cantú, Gilberto Cárdenas, Juan García
   and Christine M. Sierra, eds. *Chicana Voices: Intersections
   of Class, Race and Gender.* Austin, TX: Center for Mexican
   American Studies Publications, 1986.
Cotera, Martha P. *Diosa y Hembra, The History and Heritage of
   Chicanas in the U.S.* Austin, TX: Information Systems
   Development, 1976.
García, John A., Theresa Córdova and Juan R. García, eds. *The
   Chicano Struggle, Analyses of Past and Present Efforts.*
   Binghamton, NY: Bilingual Press/Editorial Bilingüe,
   1984.
McCluskey, Audrey T., ed. *Women of Color: Perspectives On Feminism
   and Identity.* Occasional Papers Series, Vol. 1, No. 1.
   Bloomington, IN: Women's Studies Program, Indiana
   University, 1985.
Miller, Beth, editor. *Women in Hispanic Literature, Icons and Fallen
   Idols.* Berkeley, Los Angeles, London: University of
   California Press, 1983.
Mirandé, Alfredo, and Evangelina Enríquez. *La Chicana, The
   Mexican-American Woman.* Chicago and London:
   University of Chicago Press, 1979.
Sánchez, Rosaura, and Rosa Martínez Cruz, eds. *Essays on la
   Mujer.* Los Angeles: Chicano Studies Center
   Publications, 1977.
Vásquez-Castro, Javier. *Acerca de Literatura (Diálogo Con Tres Autores*

Chicanos). Con introducción de Luis Arturo Ramos. San Antonio, TX: M&A Editions, 1979.

XI. Special Issues on Chicanas (Include Critical Literature)

De Colores. 2:3 (1975).
De Colores. 4:3 (1978).
Frontiers. "Chicanas en el Ambiente Nacional/Chicanas in the National Landscape." (Summer 1980).

XII. Reference Books and Bibliographies (General, Include Some Women's Literature)

Cabello-Argandona, Roberto, Juan Gómez-Quiñones and Patricia Herrera Durán, eds. *The Chicana: A Comprehensive Bibliographic Study.* Los Angeles: Bibliographic Research and Development Unit, Chicano Studies Center, University of California, Los Angeles, 1975.
Eger, Ernestina N. *A Bibliography of Contemporary Chicano Literature.* Berkeley: Chicano Studies Library Publications, 1982.
Martínez, Julio A., and Francisco A. Lomelí, eds. *Chicano Literature, A Reference Guide.* Westport, CT, London: Greenwood Press, 1985.
Portillo, Cristina, Graciela Ríos and Martha Rodríguez, eds. *Bibliography of Writings on La Mujer.* Berkeley: Chicano Studies Library, University of California, Berkeley, 1976.
Rodríguez, Andrés and Roberto G. Trujillo, eds. *Literatura Chicana: Creative and Critical Writings Through 1984.* Oakland, CA: Floricanto Press, 1985.
Tatum, Charles M. *Chicano Literature.* Boston: Twayne Publishers, 1982.

Peggy Job

Narradoras mexicanas contemporáneas: 1970-1987

Los datos aquí presentados son los que he podido compilar hasta la fecha. Provienen de muchas fuentes, y por lo tanto, están incompletos. Sin embargo, una lista tan extensa no existe en ninguna parte, y su utilidad para las interesadas en la literatura femenina es indudable, a pesar de sus debilidades. Las escritoras escriben en varios géneros, y unas han publicado antes de 1970; la lista consiste únicamente en su narrativa publicada entre las fechas señaladas. Así, por ejemplo, ni la bibliografía de Rosario Castellanos ni la de Elena Poniatowska están completas. No obstante, la intención es mantenernos al día. Como verán la conocida editorial Joaquín Mortiz tiene una historia ejemplar en su publicación de mujeres, por eso vale la pena inundarla con solicitudes para copias múltiples para utilizar en las aulas de estudio, así apoyando la publicación de autoras mexicanas en el futuro.

Alegría, Juana Armanda. *Diálogo prohibido*. México: Ediciones Contraste, 1985.
Argudin, Yolanda. *Moira*. México: La Gargola, 1979.
Arredondo, Inés. *Río Subterráneo*. México: Joaquín Mortiz, 1979.
_____. *Opus 123*. México: Editorial Oasis, 1983.
Bermúdez, María Elvira. *Alegoría presuntuosa*. México: Fed. Editorial Mexicana, 1971.
_____. *Cuentos herejes*. México: Oasis, 1984.
_____. *Detente, sombra*. México: Universidad Autónoma Metropolitana, 1984.
_____. *Muerte a la zaga*. México: Secretaría de Educación Publica, 1986.
_____. *Encono de hormigas*. Xalapa: Univ. Veracruzana, 1987.
Berúmen, Patricia, Oralba Castillo, Patricia Gómez M., Paloma Jiménez, y Bernarda Solís. *Sin permiso*. México: Editorial Domés, 1984.
Boullosa, Carmen. *Mejor desaparece*. México: Océano, 1987.

Campos, Julieta. *Tiene los cabellos rojizos y se llama Sabina*. México: Joaquín Mortiz, 1974.
_____. *El miedo de perder a Eurídice*. México: Joaquín Mortiz, 1979.
Careaga, Delfina. *Muñeca vestida de azul*. México: Editorial Samo, 1975.
_____. *Cosas del tiempo y otros fantasmas*. Toluca: Ediciones del Gobierno del Estado de México, 1984.
_____. *Alquimia*. Toluca: Universidad Autónoma del Estado de Mexico, 1984.
Castellanos, Rosario. *Album de familia*. México: Joaquín Mortiz, 1971.
Castillo Nájera, Oralba. *Perfume de gardenias*. México: Editorial Domés, 1982.
Clavel, Ana. *Fuera de escena*. México: Secretaría de Educación Pública/C.R.E.A., 1984.
Daltón, Margarita. *Al calor de la semilla*. n.p., 1970.
Dávila, Amparo. *Arboles petrificados*. México: Joaquín Mortiz, 1977.
Dornbierer, Manú. *La grieta y otros cuentos*. México: Editorial Diana, 1978.
_____. *El bien y el mal*. México: Océano, 1986.
Dueñas, Guadalupe. *Pasos en la escalera: La extraña visita; Girándula*. México: Editorial Porrúa, 1973.
_____. *No moriré del todo*. México: Joaquín Mortiz, 1976.
_____. *Imaginaciones*. México: Jus, 1977.
Espejo, Beatriz. *La otra hermana*. n.p. n.d.
_____. *Muros de azoque*. México: Editorial Diógenes, 1979.
Fernández, Adela. *Duermevelas*. México: Editorial Katún, 1986.
Fernández de Alba, Luz. *Boca de la necesidad*. México: Océano, l987.
Galeana, Benita. *El peso mocho*. México: Extemporáneos, 1979.
Gargallo, Francesca. *Días sin casura*. México: Leega, 1986.
Elena, Garro. *Andamos huyendo Lola*. México: Joaquín Mortiz, 1980.
_____. *Testimonios sobre Mariana*. México, Editorial Grijalbo, 1980.
_____. *La casa junto al río*. México: Grijalbo, 1982.
_____. *Reencuentro de personajes*. México: Editorial Grijalbo, 1982.
Garza Quesada, Lourdes. *Corazones no sabemos*. México: Costa-Amic Editorial, 1982.

Glantz Margo. *Las mil y una calorías, novela dietética,* Puebla: Premia, 1978.
_____. *No pronunciarás.* n.p., 1980.
_____. *Las genealogías.* México: Martín Casillas, 1981.
_____. *Dos cientas ballenas azules...y...cuatro caballos.* México: Universidad Nacional Autónoma de México, 1981.
_____. *Síndroma de naufragios.* México: Joaquín Mortiz, 1984.
_____. *De la amorosa inclinación a enredarse en cabellos.* México: Océano, 1984.
Harmony, Olga. *Letras vencidas.* n.p. 1977.
_____. *Los limones.* Xalapa: Univ. Veracruzana, 1984.
Huacuja, Malu. *Crimen sin falta de ortografía.* México: Plaza y Janés, 1986.
Hernández, Luisa Josefina. *Nostalgia de Troya.* México: Secretaría de Educación Pública, 1970 y 1986.
_____. *Los trovadores.* México: Joaquín Mortiz, 1973.
_____. *Apostasía.* n.p., 1978.
_____. *Apocalipsis cum figuris.* Xalapa: Univ. Veracruzana, 1982.
_____. *Carta de navegaciones submarinas.* México: Fondo de Cultura Económica, 1987.
Jacobs, Barbara. *Un justo acuerdo.* México: La Máquina de Escribir, 1979.
_____. *Doce cuentos en contra.* México: Martín Casillas, 1982.
_____. *Escrito en el tiempo.* México: Era, 1985.
Krauze, Ethel. *Niñas.* México: Ediciones Limusa, 1982.
_____. *Intermedio para mujeres.* México: Océano, 1982.
_____. *Donde las cosas vuelan.* México: Océano, 1985.
_____. *Nana María.* n.p., 1987.
_____. *El lunes te amaré.* México: Océano, 1987.
Leñero, Carmen. *Birlibirloque.* México: Fondo de Cultura Económica, 1987.
Loaeza, Guadalupe. *Las niñas bien.* México: Océano, 1987.
López González, Aralia, *Novela para una carta.* México: Editorial Samo, 1975.
_____. *Sema o las voces.* México: El Tucán de Virginia, 1987.
Mairena, Ana. *Cena de cenizas.* México: Joaquín Mortiz, 1975.
Mansour, Mónica. *Mala memoria.* México: Oasis, 1984.
Maqueo, Ana María. *Crimen de color oscuro.* México: Editorial Offset, 1986.
Martínez Gamba, Magaly. *Los filos.* México: El Tucán de Virginia, 1981

Mastretta, Angeles. *Arráncame la vida.* México: Océano, 1986.
Mendoza, María Luisa. *Con él, conmigo, con nosotros tres.* México: Joaquín Mortiz, 1971.
_____. *De Ausencia.* México: Joaquín Mortiz, 1974.
_____. *El perro de la escribana.* México: Joaquín Mortiz, 1982.
_____. *Ojos de papel volando.* México: n.p., n.d.
Molina, Silvia. *La mañana debe seguir gris.* México: Joaquín Mortiz, 1977.
_____. *Leyenda en la tortuga.* n.p., 1981.
_____. *Ascensión tun.* México: Martín Casillas, 1981.
Moreno, Hortensia. *Las líneas de la mano.* México: Boldó, Climent, 1985.
Muñiz, Angelina. *Morada interior.* México: Joaquín Mortíz, 1972.
_____. *Tierra adentro.* México: Joaquín Mortiz, 1977.
_____. *La guerra del unicornio.* México: Artífice, 1984.
_____. *Huerto cerrado, huerto sellado.* México: Editorial Oasis, 1985.
Neymet, Mónica de. *Las horas vivas.* México: Grijalbo, 1985.
Osorio, Lilia. *Palimpsesto.* México: Universidad Nacional Autónoma de México, 1981.
Cristina, Pacheco. *Para vivir aquí.* México: Editorial Grijalbo, 1982.
_____. *Sopita de fideo.* México: Océano, 1984.
_____. *Zona de desastre.* México: Océano, 1986.
_____. *Cuarto de azotea.* México: Gernika/Secretaría de Educación Pública, 1986.
_____. *La última noche del 'Tigre'.* México: Océano, 1987.
Pettersson, Aline. *Círculos.* México: Universidad Nacional Autónoma de México, 1977.
_____. *Casi en silencio.* Puebla: Premia, 1980.
_____. *Proyectos de muerte.* México: Martín Casillas, 1983.
_____. *Sombra ella misma.* Xalapa: Univ. Veracruzana, 1986.
_____. *Los colores ocultos.* México: Editorial Grijalbo, 1986.
Poniatowska, Elena. *Querido Diego, te abraza Quiela.* México: Era, 1978.
_____. *De noche vienes.* México: Era, 1979.
Prieto, Emma. *Los testigos.* México: Editorial Katún, 1985.
Puga, María Luisa. *Las posibilidades del odio.* México: Siglo XXI, 1978.
_____. *Cuando el aire es azul.* México: Siglo XXI, 1980.
_____. *Accidentes.* México: Martín Casillas, 1981.
_____. *Pánico o peligro.* México, Siglo XXI, 1983.

_____. *La forma del silencio.* México: Siglo XXI, 1987.
_____. *Intentos.* México: Editorial Grijalbo, 1987.
_____. (con Mónica Mansour): *Itinerario de palabras.* México: Folios Ediciones, 1987.
Puglia, Mercedes. *Prisioneros del silencio.* México: Prom. del Arte y la Cultura, 1981.
_____. *El holocausto de la primavera.* México: Editorial Diana, 1985.
Rábago Palafox, Gabriela. *Todo ángel es terrible.* México: Martín Casillas, 1981.
Rioja, Carmina. *Mágicamente.* México: Leega, 1986.
Robles, Martha. *Memorias de la libertad.* México: C.Cía. Gen. de Edic., 1979.
_____. *Los octubres de otoño.* México: Océano, 1982.
Rodríguez, Julia. *Sonata triste y otros cuentos.* México: Universidad Nacional Autónoma de México, 1985.
Rosenzweig, Carmen. *Esta cardena vida.* México: Avelar Hermanos, 1975.
_____. *Simone, el desierto: Simone, el huerto.* Toluca: Colegio de Letras, 1979.
_____. *Volanteo.* México: Cuad. Cara a Cara, 1984.
Rueda, Emma. *Cómo evitar el suicidio.* México: Fed. Edit. Mex., 1977.
Ruvinskis, Miriam. *La sala de partos verdes.* n.p., 1971.
_____. *Desde el polvo de un espejo.* n.p., 1973.
_____. *La bóveda de los címbalos.* n.p., 1982.
_____. *El cuerpo del disfraz.* n.p., 1983.
_____. *El aullido crepitante de una dama nostálgica.* Puebla: Premia, 1985.
Sauvedo Saleme, Rosaura. *Mi prima Daniela.* México: Joaquín Mortiz, 1986.
Sedeño, Livia. *Los gnomos no tienen bibliotecas.* México: Injuve, 1983.
_____. *En tiempo de marzo, en tiempo de abril.* México: Tierra Adentro, 1980.
_____. *Pie de labio ausente.* México: Editorial Katún, 1986.
Seligson, Esther. *Otros son los sueños.* México: Novaro, 1973.
_____. *Tránsito del cuerpo.* Mexico: La Máquina de Escribir, 1977.
_____. *Luz de dos.* México: Joaquín Mortiz, 1978.
_____. *De sueños, presagios y otras voces.* México: Universidad Nacional Autónoma de México, 1978.

_____. *Diálogos con el cuerpo*. México: Artífice, 1981.
_____. *La morada en el tiempo*. México: Artífice, 1981.
_____. *Sed de mar*. México. Artífice, 1986.
Urbina, Cecilia. *Las locuras breves*. México: Editorial Diana, 1986.
Valencia, Tita. *Minotauromaquia*. México: Joaquín Mortiz, 1976.
Vicens, Josefina. *Los años falsos*. México: Martín Casillas, 1982.
Vilalta, Maruxa. *El otro día, la muerte*. México: Joaquín Mortiz, 1974.
Villagarica, Rocio y Berúmen Patricia. *Carlota*. México: Editorial Diana, 1977.
Wein, Susana. *En tiempo mexicano...cuentos húngaros*. México, Editorial Katún, 1985.

Antologías de cuentos

De Llanera, Elsa. ed. *14 mujeres escriben cuentos*. México: Fed. Esc. México, 1979.
Ocampo, Aurora. ed. *Cuentistas mexicanas Siglo XX*. México: Universidad Nacional Autónoma de México, 1976.
Sefchovich, Sara. ed. *Mujeres en espejo 1*. México: Editorial Folios, 1983.
_____. *Mujeres en espejo 2*. México: Editorial Folios, 1983.
Silva Velázquez, Caridad L. y Nora Erro-Orthman. eds. *Puerta abierta. La nueva escritora latinoamericana*. México: Joaquín Mortiz, 1987.

Contributors

ADELA ALONSO was born and raised in Mexico and is now living in Central Texas. She is of the opinion that "Writing, like sex, is a scary and exciting process of self-discovery, full of contradictions and mixed feelings, but well worth it. We change ourselves, we change those around us, until nothing is ever the same."

ELVIA ALVARADO is an Honduran woman who, as the subtitle of her book states "Speaks from the Heart." The story of Elvia Alvarado was translated and edited by Medea Benjamin, A Food First Book, the Institute for Food and Development Policy, San Francisco, 1987.

CECILIA ALVAREZ has exhibited her work in Mexico, the United States and Europe. She has received the 1987 Certificate of Recognition from the City of Seattle where she resides. Her artistic objectives include the exploration of the multilevel realities not acknowledged by mainstream American existence and art.

JULIA ALVAREZ was born in New York City and spent her early childhood in the Dominican Republic. She is the author of a book of poems, *Homecoming* (Grove Press, 1984), and many short stories. She teaches Creative Writing at the University of Illinois.

GLORIA ANZALDÚA is a Texan now living in California's Bay Area. She is the co-editor of *This Bridge Called My Back* (1981), and more recently published a collection of prose and poetry, *Borderlands/La Frontera: The New Mestiza* (Spinsters/Aunt Lute, 1987).

SANTA BARRAZA is influenced by the border culture of Texas where she was raised. She has an MA in Art from the University of Texas, Austin. She is currently professor of Art at the University of La Roche in Pittsburgh, PA.

ANA CASTILLO is a native of Chicago and lives in California's Bay Area. She has published two collections of poetry *Women Are Not Roses* (Arte Público Press, 1984) and *My Father Was A Toltec* (West

End Press, 1988); and a novel, *The Mixquiahuala Letters* (Bilingual Press, 1986).

CORDELIA CHÁVEZ CANDELARIA teaches Chicano and English literature at the University of Colorado, Boulder and is the author of a collection of poetry *Ojo de la cueva/Cave Springs* (Maize Press, 1984), and a book of critical essays, *Chicano Poetry: An Introduction* (Greenwood Press, 1986).

DENISE CHÁVEZ is a native of New Mexico and teaches Dramatic Arts and Creative Writing at the University of Houston. Her most recent book is *The Last of the Menu Girls* (Arte Público Press, 1986), and her work in progress includes the novel *The Face of an Angel.*

RITA CHÁVEZ resides in Seattle. Her work has been exhibited in the United States and Europe.

SANDRA CISNEROS is a native of Chicago and has set up residence in Texas. Her books include *The House on Mango Street* (Arte Público Press, 1984, rev. ed. 1988), and a book of poetry *My Wicked Wicked Ways* (Third Woman Press, 1987).

CLAUDIA COLINDRES es salvadoreña genéticamente, guatemalteca de nacimiento, mexicana de corazón, puertorriqueña por casualidad, chicana en ideología y minoría de los Estados Unidos por obligación. Espera graduarse de UC Berkeley en 1989 con un Bachillerato en Chicano Studies.

LUCHA CORPI is a Chicana poet residing in the Bay Area. She is the author of *Palabras de Mediodia/Noon Words* and the novel *Delia's Song* (Arte Público Press, 1988).

ROSINA CONDE is a native of Mexicali, Baja California. She has published two collections of stories, *De infancia y adolescencia* (Panfleto y Pantomima, 1982) and *En la tarima* (Universidad Autónoma Metropolitana, Laberinto, 1984); and a collection of poetry, *Poemas de seducción* (La Máquina de escribir, 1981).

BARBARA BRINSON CURIEL was born and raised in San Francisco. A poet, critic and translator, she teaches Creative Writing at the University of California, Santa Cruz. "Ciudadano de mis sueños" appears in her most recent collection of poems *Speak To Me From Dreams* (Third Woman Press, 1989).

ERLINDA GONZÁLES-BERRY is professor of Latin American and Chicano Literature at the University of New Mexico. She has published widely on Chicano/a literature and has just finished a novel, *Paletitas de guayaba*, from which the excerpt appearing in *Third Woman* has been taken.

ROSALEE GURROLA is a native of California. Her work has been published in *Shattersheet* (Los Angeles) and is presently working on a collection of poetry, *On Channel Zero*.

MARINA GUTIÉRREZ is a native of New York where she presently lives. Her work has been exhibited in New York, Canada and the Caribbean. A lot of her work is committed to the representation of Third World women.

ESTER HERNÁNDEZ was born and raised in Dinuba in the central San Joaquín Valley of California where she spent her early years as a farmworker. Her work includes prints, serigraphs and pastels depicting the beauty, dignity, strength, experiences, and dreams of Raza women. She has exhibited in the United States, Mexico, and England.

JUANA ALICIA is a Chicana artist residing in San Francisco. She is a muralist, illustrator, painter and lithographer. She states that her "work reflects her historical and cultural matrix and consciously addresses the inherent conflicts in being a minority woman within this society."

PEGGY JOB is a doctoral candidate in Latin American Literature at the University of New South Wales, Sydney, Australia. She did field work in Mexico during 1986-87 with the aid of a fellowship from the Mexican Secretaría de Relaciones Exteriores and from the Australian Government. Her work has been carried out with the support of the Programa Interdisciplinario de Estudios de la Mujer at the Colegio de México under the direction of Professor Elena Urrutia.

JUANITA LUNA LAWHN is a native of Texas and professor of

English at San Antonio College. Her current research is concerned with the women of *La Prensa*, 1913-1957.

CHERRÍE MORAGA is a native of Los Angeles and coeditor of *This Bridge Called My Back* (1981). She is the author of a collection of essays, stories, and poems entitled *Loving in the War Years* (South End Press, 1983), and a play *Giving Up the Ghost* (West End Press, 1986).

ARCELIA PONCE is a first-year student at the University of California, Berkeley. The piece presented here is one that she wrote for a Chicano Studies English Composition class.

ALVINA E. QUINTANA is a holder of the Chicana Dissertation Fellowship at the University of California, Santa Barbara, 1988-89. She has taught at Raza Studies at San Francisco State as well as the University of California, Santa Cruz. She has been a member of the editorial collective of *Revista Mujeres* (Santa Cruz).

SONIA RIVERA-VALDÉS was born in Cuba and lives in New York. She teaches at Fordham University and devotes her time to the study of contemporary Cuban women writers and cinematographers.

VICTORIA ALEGRÍA ROSALES is a native of Mexico now residing in the California Bay Area. She is a novelist and poet currently finishing her MA in Creative Writing, Spanish Literature and Women's Studies at San Francisco State. The title of her novel in progress is *Entre Angélica y Manuel*.

ANA MARÍA SIMO was born in Cuba and resides in New York. She recently finished *Love Confused*, a musical commissioned by INTAR for the 1988 New York International Theatre Festival. She is the author of *Passion, Dungeon* and *Exiles* as well as other plays.

MARY SIQUEIROS is a retired working woman and mother. The pieces printed in this volume were presented at a writing workshop for Chicanas in Watsonville, California. The "First Time," was generated through a "meditation writing exercise," and "My Other Self" is an excerpt from her journal.

CARMEN TAFOLLA is originally from San Antonio, Texas and currently resides in Arizona. She is the author of three books of poetry, children's books and screenplays, as well as a collection of essays on Chicanas *To Split a Human* (Mexican American Cultural Center, San Antonio, TX, 1985). Her latest manuscript *Sonnets to Human Beings* won First Prize in the University of California at Irvine National Chicano Literary Competition.

LOURDES TORRES teaches Linguistics at SUNY, Stoneybrook. Her research includes the literature of U.S. Latinos.

LUZ MARÍA UMPIERRE teaches Caribbean and Latin American Literature at Rutgers University. She is a critic and poet. Her critical works include *Ideología y novela en Puerto Rico* and *Nuevas aproximaciones críticas a la literatura puertorriqueña contemporánea*. Her poetry collections include *Y otras desgracias/And Other Misfortunes* (Third Woman Press, 1985) and *The Margarita Poems* (Third Woman Press, 1987).

ENEDINA CÁSAREZ VÁSQUEZ is a native of San Antonio, Texas. For her work she has received the Hidalgo de Béyar Prize and the Marguerite Davenport Humanities Prize. She has been nominated to the San Antonio Women's Hall of Fame and serves on the Art and Culture Advisory Committee for the city of San Antonio. She is the author of *Recuerdos de una niña*.

SYLVIANA WOOD is an actress, director and playwright. She has developed for performance a variety of characters and stories including the much-liked Doña Chona, V.M.B. (Vieja Mitotera del Barrio).

YVONNE YARBRO-BEJARANO teaches Spanish and Chicano Literature at the University of Washington. She has published widely on Chicano Theater and is currently at work on the honor plays of the Golden Age from a feminist perspective.

Books available from Third Woman Press

CHICANA LESBIANS: THE GIRLS OUR MOTHERS WARNED US ABOUT edited by Carla Trujillo. Winner of numerous awards, including the Lambda Literary Award for Best Lesbian Anthology. ISBN 0-943219-06-X, $10.95

CHICANA CRITICAL ISSUES, edited by the MALCS editorial board. The highly recommended first anthology in a new series of Chicana/Latina studies. ISBN 0-943219-09-4, $14.95

NEIGHBORS by Joan Woodruff. A magical and compelling novel set in New Mexico, by the author of *Traditional Stories and Foods: An American Indian Remembers*. ISBN 0-943219-08-6, $11.95

CHILIAGONY by Iris Zavala, translated by Susan Pensak. This Puertorriqueña's famous short novel is a work of "fabulous inventions and mental witchcraft." ISBN 0-943219-02-3, $5.95

MY WICKED WICKED WAYS by Sandra Cisneros. Now in its third printing, this book by the author of *The House on Mango Street* and *Women Hollering Creek* is the most famous, and infamous, collection of Chicana poetry. ISBN 0-943219-01-9, $8.95

VARIACIONES SOBRE UNA TEMPESTAD by Lucha Corpi, translated by Catherine Rodríguez-Nieto. Poetry from the acclaimed and prize-winning poet (*Palabras de mediodía*) and novelist (*Eulogy For a Brown Angel*). Bilingual, Spanish and English. ISBN 0-943219-05-1, $8.95

THE MARGARITA POEMS by Luz María Umpierre-Herrera. Intensely personal and moving poetry from the author of *Y Otras Desgracias/And Other Misfortunes*. Puerto Rico's most outstanding poet and essayist. ISBN 0-943219-02-7, $5.95

SPEAK TO ME FROM DREAMS by Barbara Brinson Curiel. Rich, evocative poetry from the author of *Nocturno* and *Vocabulary of the Dead* that captures the essence of growing up Chicana. ISBN 0-943219-03-5, $8.95

Back issues of THIRD WOMAN journal still available at $8.95 each: TW3 *Texas and More*; TW2:2 *International Perspectives*; TW2:1 *Southwest/Midwest*

Also available through Third Woman Press:
ESTA PUENTE, MI ESPALDA: VOCES DE MUJERES TERCERMUNDISTAS EN LOS ESTADOS UNIDOS edited by Cherríe Moraga and Ana Castillo. The Spanish adaptation and translation of the best-selling *This Bridge Called My Back: Writings by Radical Women of Color*. ISBN 0-910383-19-7. $10.00

Send for a free catalog. For all orders please add $1.50 for the first book and $.50 for each additional book. California residents add state and local sales tax. Make checks payable to Third Woman Press. Send to: Third Woman Press, Ethnic Studies, Dwinelle Hall 3412, University of California, Berkeley, CA 94720.